André Malraux: The Conquest of Dread

Gerda Blumenthal

ANDRÉ
MALRAUX

the conquest of dread

145006 GREENWOOD PRESS, PUBLISHERS
WESTPORT, CONNECTICUT

Library of Congress Cataloging in Publication Data

Blumethal, Gerda, 1923–
  André Malraux : the conquest of dread.

  Reprint of the ed. published by Johns Hopkins Press,
Baltimore.
  Includes index.
  1. Malraux, André, 1901–1976--Criticism and interpre-
tation. 2. Light and darkness in literature.
PQ2625.A716Z6 1979   843'.9'12   78-12576
ISBN 0-313-21194-9

© 1960 by The Johns Hopkins Press, Baltimore 18, Md.

Reprinted with the permission of The Johns Hopkins University
Press

Reprinted in 1979 by Greenwood Press, Inc.,
51 Riverside Avenue, Westport, CT 06880

Printed in the United States of America

10 9 8 7 6 5 4 3 2 1

Contents

Introduction

The realm of the sacred which has never relinquished its hold on Malraux has two poles: darkness and light, the demonic and the divine, desolation and communion; one arouses horror, the other love. In his poetic and most revealing essay on Goya, Malraux points to the great Spanish artist's obsession with the powers of darkness as the mainspring of his life's work. To have found one's language, as Goya found his when illness, deafness, and anguish made him finally break away from the graceful tradition of the eighteenth century, does not mean that one is able to say all things. What Goya had to say, in his nightmarish series of etchings, "Mirrors," "Disasters," or "Don't Awaken Them," or in the ghoulish painting, "Saturn," was that human destiny and, in particular, his personal destiny were prey to all the demons and monsters of hell and to the night of an irremediable despair and loneliness. In order not to be utterly possessed and destroyed by that fateful darkness, he spent his life seeking to master it, as did Gérard de Nerval and after him Baudelaire and now Malraux himself, by fixing and accusing it in symbol and image. This has throughout the ages been one of the achievements of art:

Introduction

to exorcise the powers of night and deliver the artist
and those of his time and situation from their grip and
fascination.

It is the purpose of this study to show the presence of
the saturnine element, that dark, alien counterpart of the
divine, in all of Malraux's work, and to reveal its gradual
transformation from an autonomous and all-determining
force into one that is mastered and brought into creative
relation to the human and the divine. In the works up to
1930, it will be seen as the element that absolutely dominates and shapes every major character, action, and image.

The world in *The Conquerors (Les Conquérants)* and
The Royal Way (La Voie Royale) is essentially a world of
stones, specters, and demons. Its solitary, foredoomed adven-
turers who set out to challenge this world in a grim dialogue are fated to come to resemble the very destiny they
seek to subdue. It is as Garcia says in *Man's Hope (L'Espoir)*,
"In every war each side adopts the characteristics of the
enemy, whether they wish it or not."[1] In their lonely Promethean struggle for self-assertion in the face of fate's destructive indifference, they find themselves separated from the
gods, from the world and from their own selves, and become
ultimately unrecognizable, silenced, devoured. It is a world
of masks, a world held captive by the concealing false masks
of legend and an impersonality born out of self-hatred and
despair. In each of those early novels, Saturn triumphs
after a holocaust that is like the Christmas carnival in Kazan
in 1919 which haunts Garine's memory in *The Conquerors*

[1] André Malraux, *Man's Hope,* trans. Stuart Gilbert and Alastair Macdonald (New York: Random House, 1938), p. 506. In this study I shall give
all quotations from the texts in English, either taking them from published
translations or using my own.

—with the difference that it is a holocaust of men, not of gods. When the masks are wrenched away in the final agony, nothing is seen underneath but the hostile, aloof stare of the condemned.

In the novels of the following thirteen years, *Man's Fate (La Condition Humaine)*, *The Days of Wrath (Le Temps du Mépris)*, *Man's Hope (L'Espoir)*, and *The Walnut Trees of Altenburg (Les Noyers de l'Altenburg)*, the saturnine remains a powerfully marked and indeed dominant presence, but it is no longer absolute master of the scene. In the very midst and out of a universe of darkness, imprisonment, and seemingly hopeless alienation, mysteriously privileged moments and beings are born. They rise above the inhuman silence of derision and despair, and burst into a pure song of human grief and ecstasy; human faces become visible in flickers of light; at the same time the impersonality of myth and adventure, assuming in frenzied moments the rigid aspect of pseudo divinity, gives way to an impersonality achieved slowly, painfully, in a process of true human growth and self-transcendence. No longer Prometheus doomed by the gods and his own pride, but a human being in a frail and humble communion with other human beings emerges as the protagonist, as the challenger of fate.

Gradually we see the death-bound will to individual self-assertion transform itself into a creative, if ever tragic, affirmation of human dignity and communion. These works still confront us with a world of strangers, a world forever sinking into a deep pit, a world that is dark, cruel, and seemingly absurd in its writhings and its poor derided dreams of justice and fulfillment. At the same time, moments of a mysterious twilight reveal, among the anguished grimaces of the defeated, glimpses of the "eternal mask" of that other death that spells a consummation. There is the death of those few who, through lucidity and sacrifice, have achieved victory over terror and despair. They die after having broken the chains of solitude, not only for themselves but for all those who have witnessed their struggle and their end. They have given a voice to all those who are silenced by dread and unconsciousness. This voice dominates the ghastly silence of Saturn; it releases the frozen attitudes of despair and gives new life and new mobility to human compassion and hope, as fundamental in man, and as essential to him, as his dread, once dread is conquered.

Up to *The Walnut Trees of Altenburg,* all Malraux's novels revolve around political and revolutionary action. *The Walnut Trees* is a work of transition, framing a philosophical meditation on art by two narratives of war. It is hardly a novel. The great works that follow it, most notably *Saturn (Saturne)* and *The Voices of Silence (Les Voix du Silence),* indicate a turning away from fiction. They translate for us, in a luminous and massive exposition, Malraux's vision of art and furnish us with a major key to a proper approach to his own works of fiction. More clearly even than in the novels, Malraux, in these critical studies, proceeds by identification. This is not so much to say that he is subjective in his dealing with artistic and cultural problems as that he chooses, or feels compelled, to clarify and define those problems and elements of life around which gravitate and on which hinge his own life and art, and that he does not concern himself at all with what is totally alien to him. M. Gaëtan Picon has pointed this out in his beautiful study on Malraux.[2]

2 *Malraux par lui-même* (Paris: Aux Editions du Seuil, 1953).

While he has never ceased to play an active role on the political scene, Malraux the artist has turned his attention away from the purely historical realm of political action to art, always his truest and most perfect medium of insight, self-realization and creation. Yet, as this study will attempt to show, the focal point of his entire creative work has been the same, from the early revolutionary novels to the recent meditations in *La Métamorphose des Dieux;* namely the haunting concern to define man's role in the dialogue between the human and the sacred.

The essays on art have grown out of a persistent and arduous effort on this poet's part to apply and clarify his vision of man's fate—not only in speculative and esthetic activity but in heeding the pressing exigencies of the moment through political action. As twentieth-century history has been a succession of Saturnalia, this was not only politically but also artistically most fruitful, in offering to an essentially nocturnal and tragic temperament and vision the darkest of scenes for the fashioning of a style. But purely historical action, while fighting the blind determinisms of fate, proved to Malraux to be in itself too largely governed by mechanical and destructive laws to constitute man's ultimate challenge to Saturn.[3] Art too accuses, as does political rebellion; but in accusing, it is not caught in the closed dialectic that traps those who by committing themselves entirely to the dictates of the self like Perken *(The Royal Way),* or to the historical moment like Garine, have hoped to transcend the self and the moment.

[3] Cf. André Malraux, "Aftermath of the Absolute," *The Voices of Silence,* trans. Stuart Gilbert (Garden City: Doubleday, 1953).

In art, rebellion is creative;[4] it challenges the present, it redeems the past through its power of metamorphosis, securing it in a chain of creative filiations; it creates the vision that ensures future rebellion and transformation; and so it belongs to duration, and not merely to time. Political action is of the moment and suffers tragic and inevitable degradation in time; in smiting one face of Saturn, it resurrects another, possibly no less hideous. In artistic creation, through the mystery of style, darkness is not merely challenged, it is transfigured. It becomes the true, dynamic counterpart of what is symbolized by the golden background of the Byzantine mosaics; or, in Malraux's words, "it is not only dark, it is also the night,"[5] that is, eternal counterpart of an eternal day. There is no magic in Malraux's imagination, no sleight of metaphor that will turn bloody Saturn into a god of love. But there is the hope, man's most fundamental hope, that if the menace of doom and despair can be mastered in man's heart and soul, his destiny may then be free to encounter and be encompassed once again by a radiance that might bear resemblance to the smile of Rheims, to be sustained and transfigured anew.

[4] Camus, whose evolution paralleled Malraux's in a striking way, and who no doubt was deeply influenced by Malraux, has a brilliant final chapter on art and creative rebellion in *L'Homme révolté*.

[5] André Malraux, *Saturne: Essai sur Goya* (1st edn.; Paris: Galerie de la Pléiade, NRF, 1950), p. 55.

I

SATURNALIA

1

Mirrors and Masks of Fate

In *The Conquerors* and *The Royal Way*,[1] the silence of death rings out over a universe that is but a vast mirror of nothingness. The "nuit des astres," a sultry, leaden sky which emits a blinding glare reminiscent of Goya's "black sun,"[2] is reflected below by the "nuit terrestre": monstrous jungle life, decaying cities, and disintegrating destinies. Rather than a true battle, there is a complex and awesome correspondence between heaven and earth, between Saturn and man. The world of human endeavor and adventure is but a colorful mask under which is concealed a boundless despair, germ of inevitable ultimate annihilation.

In vain, Perken, Garine, and Hong rise in rebellion against death's too easy victory; death is within them. Their Promethean heroism reflects only a hopeless defiance of their own inner demons of terror and self-hatred. No deliverance is possible for them. Every bond they seek to estab-

[1] The first editions of these are dated, respectively, 1928 and 1930. The quotations are taken from: André Malraux, *The Conquerors*, trans. Winifred Stephens Whale (New York: Harcourt, Brace & Co., 1929); and André Malraux, *The Royal Way*, trans. Stuart Gilbert (New York: Harrison Smith and Robert Haas, 1935).

[2] André Malraux, *Saturne: Essai sur Goya* (1st edn.; Paris: Galerie de la Pléiade, NRF, 1950), p. 76.

lish with the world to lead them beyond themselves merely serves to extend their prison. There is, on the one hand, the bond of a common doom, mythical and terrible, which chains together those who refuse to submit, the solitary heroes, Garine and the narrator, Rebecci and Hong of *The Conquerors,* or Perken and Claude of *The Royal Way.* There is, on the other hand, the bond by which these men tie the world to them, seeking to transform it into a docile reflection of their power, into a multifaced mask to cover the unbearable void within them. It is a hermetic universe of correspondences and reflections in which everything, from the immutable clouds down to the sea and to the depths of the heroes' self-awareness, finds its final death-bound reality in the night that belongs to the devouring god, Saturn.

Imprisoned by an overdeveloped, painful sense of their individual distinctness, the last and dubious gift Europe has bestowed on its spiritual heirs through Nietzsche above all and the whole German romantic tradition, Malraux's rebels turn from the West with bitterness. They are drawn to the Far East, tempted by a vision of life that is incarnate in the beautiful Sung paintings and all of the great works of art that Asia has given to the world: a contemplative and sensuous vision of cosmic harmony in which the human soul merges with the universe, in which the human figure becomes one with the landscape that surrounds it. Weary with solitude, that state of irreducible separateness, they come to the Orient seeking to blot out their harsh petrified silhouettes in a soft, all-absorbing land of stillness, not by surrendering, but by taking possession of it in a way as passionate and as self-obliterating as sexual conquest. Conquest, time and again, is but a masked surrender, not to another being, but to a projection of the self, to a mirror; it is a grim mockery. The whole host of Malraux's heroes who succumb to the temptation of the Orient, from Garine to Vincent Berger in *The Walnut Trees of Altenburg*, have this experience in common: they find Asia inhuman and unbreathable, with her low skies, her oppressive heat, her monstrous vegetation, her vast, devouring jungles and deserts and crumbling temples. At the same time, they find her in a full process of cultural transformation, with her young intellectuals avidly grasping at the very notion from which they themselves are trying to free themselves as from a mortal illness—namely, the sense of uniqueness and the all-redeeming significance of a man's individual destiny.

There is a bitter and fateful irony in the encounter between the Western rebels' stony profiles and inner state of corrosion on the one hand, and Asia's outer state of dissolution and the young Turks' and Chinamen's rigid grimace of hatred and revolt on the other. Instead of a fruitful dialogue between two essential and vital visions of the world seeking to complete each other, two states of disintegration find themselves mirrored in each other in a dizzying counterpoint of stones and swamps, bleakness and glaring colors, silence and profusion of sounds, immobility and futile gestures of conquest and self-immolation.

The perfect image of this two-faced mockery of defeat is the island of Hong Kong in *The Conquerors*. Hong Kong powerfully symbolizes the obsession of the Western world to dominate the Orient. In the novel, this last stronghold of Europe, the only solid rock that stands out on the vast and mysterious Asiatic horizon, is under siege. It has turned into a ghost city. "The mass of the famous, the most formidable rock . . . veiled with a light mist, and seeming to end in the stars" gives the impression now of "something like a black world."[3] In an incantation of despair, Malraux chants of this deserted city in its nocturnal solitude, of this once-powerful island, now nothing but "a form outlined by a chain of twinkling dots, dwindling slowly as they stand out against the black sky which seems to engulf them."[4] A gaunt, black shape, it is surrounded by myriad lights in the sky and the sea, which suggest less the power of the white men who made them than "some Polynesian scene, one of those feasts in which painted gods are honored by the scattering of clouds of glowworms into the darkness."[5] Deserted by its power and its inhabitants, the city harbors within its bleak walls, as the only remaining trace of life, hospitals that have been left without doctors and nurses and are overcrowded with sick people—symbols of the city's defeat and abandonment.

The same nightmarish despair, both stony and putrid, hangs over Canton, where most of the action takes place. An oppressive heat stings the city like a wound. On the streets a strong odor of decomposition mingles with the sickly fragrance of flowers and the smell of tar and stagnant water. The ominous silence of the city alternates with the equally ominous barking sounds emitted at mass meetings by thousands of coolies who resemble dogs with their rigid inert bodies and their sudden, jerking, forward movements of approbation. Scenes in desolate streets and vacant dark corridors are succeeded by scenes of forlorn crowds in smoky

3 *The Conquerors*, p. 50.
4 *Ibid.*, p. 73.
5 *Ibid.*, p. 51.

halls; the monstrous spectacle of the tortured bodies of Klein and his three companions standing upright against the wall of the police station displaces another vision of death: the rhapsodic scene of Tcheng-Dai's funeral, in which death is celebrated in carnival fashion, with a profusion of instruments—drums, gongs, violins, flutes, bagpipes—and colors of crimson, purple, cerise, rose, vermilion, carmine—all shades of red, symbol of passion.

But it is Hong Kong, the besieged city, that has taken on the semblance of a prison. Struggling to maintain itself against its own inner corruption of wealth and power and the outer forces of rebellion, it becomes every day more like a specter of fate, silent and inhuman.

It shares this transformation with Garine, the hero of *The Conquerors*, chief of propaganda in Canton. Like Perken a *heimatlos* European, Garine has come to assume his heavy and responsible task in the Chinese revolution with the hope of leaving behind a hated world and a hated self, and of testing his powers on this, for him final, scene of battle against the two most unendurable aspects of man's absurd fate: humiliation and injustice. The narrator recalls through his personal recollections, and furthermore discovers in the secret police record on Garine, all the "successive faces" of this haunted rebel, the diverse masks of this adventurer bent on dominating and directing, while he can, the hopeless game of life. Finally his malaria, the long-subdued physical symptom of his devouring sense of tragedy and impotence, breaks out full force under the stress of the unwholesome climate and his feverish activity. It leaves Garine ravaged and imprints upon his face a masklike impenetrable quality. It finally reveals the true and only master of all the scenes of his life, the master he had tried to vanquish and to conceal through action—*la hantise de la vanité du monde.*

With bitter yet seemingly unconscious irony, the dying man confides his paradoxical secret to the narrator, the young man who witnesses his agony: "There is no power, there is not even true life without the certainty, the obsession of the futility of everything."[6] At the moment when his role can no longer mask the self-destroying and besieged self (at that very moment his action comes to fruition: the decree he has fought for, forbidding ships to refuel at Hong Kong, has been passed), Garine happens to look into the mirror. It is a symbolic gesture of defeat that recurs many times throughout Malraux's works. Merciless toward his own suffering, and after a brutal movement of his foot, as if he wanted to crush something, he takes the mirror out of his pocket and reads the certainty of death in his own reflection.[7]

Embodying now in his own hated self the fateful decay of the Orient to which he has striven to give a new shape, he has a sudden longing to return to Europe, to assert himself once more within the magic of the imperial strength of England. But it is too late for that. As for the strong, all things serve to challenge and to reflect their strength, so every thing and place and being turns into a mirror of death to the dying. While outside his window Canton is tumultuously celebrating the advance of the Cantonese army, a victory which he has so largely made possible, the darkness of final surrender has already cut him off from the world of the living, now more than ever alien and hateful to him.

Ironic destiny! It is a re-enacting, end and all, of another

[6] *Ibid.,* p. 253.
[7] *Ibid.,* p. 266.

memory that has been haunting Garine; of a gruesome, Goy-aesque scene that he witnessed during the war, a mock wedding ceremony staged by fifty or so soldiers, in which the "bride" is a young soldier new to the regiment who had boasted he would kill anyone who dared to rape him. He is firmly held by two grotesque-looking characters disguised in carnival fashion as women, and he is unable to move. The candles are extinguished, his screams are heard; he is being raped by them all. As Garine relates the scene, he wonders aloud: was there a foreboding of his fate in his reckless boast? and then remarks calmly that what obsesses him is not the end, certainly, but the absurd, parody-like beginning. When he sees his approaching death confirmed in his friend's eyes as they meet his glance, it is with calm aloofness, from across an unbridgeable chasm.

To Claude Vannec and Perken likewise, Asia promises liberation from a dreadful revulsion against life, and then reveals herself instead to be a fateful mirage, a vast and limitless reflection of their murderous inner state of defi-ance, and their deep sense of loss. Claude, the young arche-ologist, sets out to seek the ancient Royal Way in the deadly jungles of Cambodia and Siam, with its precious Khmer temples—crumbling symbols of a lost glory. He is deter-mined to "wrench his dream clear of the inert world that shackles them,"[8] ready to stake his life on this expedition to "a land possessed . . . its ancient hymns like its temples fallen on evil days; of all dead lands most dead,"[9] ready to find and resurrect the lost vision that haunts him, or perish.

[8] *The Royal Way,* p. 55.
[9] *Ibid.,* p. 71.

It is a double-faced mirror with which the forest allures him. Which is the true face, which the concealing mask?—the monstrous, stifling jungle, dangerous, swampy, swarming with insects, veritable kingdom of death; or those miracles of grace and nobility, the temples with their statuary, timeless even though held captive by the jungle and ravaged by time and the cruel sun? This expedition is like a wager, and the odds are on the side of Saturn. The timeless battle between fate and human will is re-enacted as Claude descends into this inhuman world, to be devoured by it, or to return transfigured, a god.

The pages that depict the venture into the jungle, the grim, devastating obstacles; the disillusionments every time a temple is found in ruin and void of sculptures alternating with those brief moments of ecstatic triumph when victory seems at hand in the form of priceless bas-reliefs, constitute one long epic prose poem. All earthly and heavenly powers of destruction are seen pitted against the frail power of a man's imagination and refusal to yield, and, several times, for the length of a breathless instant, they are defeated and annulled. Like rays of light these fugitive victories rift the heavy, ominous sky, only to be smothered again an instant later by the all-engulfing darkness. But these moments are timeless. They belong to the gods and to the world of legend. They bear witness to Prometheus' glorious challenge, willingly atoned for by the unending solitary agony on the rock.

The demonic power embodied by the jungle obliterates everything human, even anguish:

> Like a slow poison, the ceaseless fermentation in which forms grew bloated, lengthened out, decayed, as in a world where mankind has no place, wore down Claude's stamina

insidiously; under its influence, in the green darkness, he felt himself disintegrating like the world around him. . . . Here what act of man had any meaning, what human will but spent its staying-power? Here everything frayed out, grew soft and flabby, tended to assimilate itself with its surroundings, which, loathsome yet fascinating as a cretin's eyes, worked on the nerves with the same obscene power of attraction as the spiders hanging there between the branches, from which at first it had cost him such an effort to avert his gaze.[10]

As if under an evil spell, the senses are muted and all traces of a conscious will disintegrate. A wild, almost delirious desire to abandon himself seizes Claude. This is the ultimate place of dread, all-dissolving, all-encompassing, leaving no part of anguish free to scream out in frenzy. He feels only a profound lassitude in the face of this "universal disintegration of all things under an unseen sun,"[11] on this "phantasmal road."[12] But the will to conquer is not actually abolished—it lives in the limbs that struggle on mechanically past a succession of desolate ruins of temples. Then the miracle happens which forces the darkness to recede: following the glance of the men ahead of him who have been calling out to him, Claude suddenly sees what they see—a lovely bas-relief on the apex of a crumbled temple, almost completely concealed by the foliage:

Between the leaves he noticed a stone bird with outspread wings and a parrot's beak. A shaft of sunlight broke directly over one of its feet. All his anger (at the joyous voices of the men) vanished in that brief but splendid moment. Delight possessed him; he was filled with an aimless gratitude, with

10 *Ibid.,* pp. 101–102.
11 *Ibid.,* p. 112.
12 *Ibid.,* p. 113.

an elation which quickly yielded to a maudlin readiness to weep.[13]

The battle is not won, for these marvelous images are jealously guarded by the voracious, violent plant life that hovers over, under, and around them and by the crumbling yet powerful monsters of stone from which they have to be detached. "A presence of numinous awe guarded with its dread hand these ancient figures holding their lonely court amongst the centipedes and vermin of the forest." But Claude is not alone to claim them; Perken steps forward, "and in a flash the world of shimmering sea depths died out, like a jellyfish cast high and dry on the sea-shore; it lost potency when faced by two white men."[14] A concrete image of their dream is before Claude and Perken and the ecstatic confrontation, promising a resurrection from the death of time, makes them for a moment the equals and even the masters of the death that is within and around them. As they hammer away at the immovable stone to detach the precious reliefs— the figures of two female dancers—they hammer against a prison wall which holds captive nothing less than their lives. As the stone refuses to yield, every blow Claude strikes seems to confirm his imprisonment. Like an attack of a fatal illness, the temptation to surrender to death, reflected in the merciless jungle and its opposition to his will, comes over him: "He pictured himself, his arms hugging his chest, like a man stricken by malaria, his body curled up like a sleeping animal; he would lose consciousness utterly, yielding with sublime relief to the reiterated call of heat and jungle."[15]

13 *Ibid.*, p. 115.
14 *Ibid.*, p. 117.
15 *Ibid.*, pp. 127–28.

Then the very imminence of death summons him back to life, arousing in him a violent movement of anger against this cruel, taunting mockery, which he seems to hear in the snickering of the monkeys overhead. In a state of madness he hammers on and finally forces the wall to release its treasure. The sculptured surface of the huge blocks comes off. Once more, for a short spell, as if by magic, the forest is transfigured from a hostile menace into his equal, his ally: "Thanks to the fallen stone he was suddenly in harmony with the forest and the temple."[16] For an instant only; then Saturn's laughter resounds anew over the universe, to crush the mocked fool: there is no way of transporting the sculptures to safety. Useless agony; the promise was but a temptation after all, a mask of light, to lure him into the evil land of no return.

There is a deep significance in Claude and Perken's failure to retrieve the statues from destruction. For theirs is not a pure quest. Unlike the voyage of the "Bateau Ivre" and its descent into hell to recapture the azure and the flaming suns of a lost golden age, the venture of the heroes of *The Royal Way* is stained because it is a quest for power. The statues, to them, constitute power; they are means of acquiring wealth. Unconsciously in Claude's case, but explicitly with Perken, the quest is saturnine in that it is born out of rebellion and the need to destroy; and so it carries within it the germ of defeat. There is this essential difference between Malraux and his heroes, Perken in particular: they are not poets. The moving force that draws them recklessly to the realm of dread is not so much a passionate longing for the treasure as it is their dread itself, which is so

16 *Ibid.*, p. 131.

powerful that it imprisons the treasure when it is found. The soul of Perken in whom Claude has recognized his prototype and who becomes the leader in the expedition is too frozen with despair to open to the "azure"; it can only burst asunder in an ecstasy of destruction. It has no life to impart, no true power to resurrect. As Perken seeks to exorcise blind fatality from himself and impose it upon the world in the form of his will to conquer, there is only the gradual disintegration of hopes, beings, and forms, his own above all, into fragments and masks of petrified defiance.

When Claude first meets Perken in a brothel in Djibouti and then observes him on board the ship that is taking them to Indochina, he is fascinated and troubled by him, by the air of mystery that surrounds him. An evil rumor will have it that Perken needs vast sums of money for dubious, disreputable purposes. "More potent than the menace of the jungle, that 'Perken legend,' ill-natured, doubtless, yet somewhat grandiose, was working on Claude like a ferment, like the darkness all around him, disintegrating all that he had deemed the real world."[17] Perken begins to obsess him. He watches Perken's face which he sees as a silhouette in the shadow, enigmatic and unapproachable, and listens spellbound to his voice which is tinged with irony and has a magical, legendary quality. No one around Perken escapes the magic that emanates from him; it stirs the crowd and arouses its trivial imagination; it makes those who are in his presence instinctively lower their voices in acknowledgment of his unspoken mastery. An anguished curiosity pushes Claude to him, "as if this man prefigured his own destiny,"[18]

[17] *Ibid.*, p. 37.
[18] *Ibid.*, p. 19.

and compels him to discover the nature of their strange affinity.

Memories of his grandfather rise up in Claude's mind and establish a link with this stranger's presence, to form a "twofold, reiterated menace, haunting as two parallel prognostications."[19] Do they not both belong to the "race maudite," that unhappy race which "knew better than any men on earth the burden and the bitterness of life and the dark powers that govern it"?[20] All his grandfather's life had been one continuous gesture of disgust with his existence and disdain for those who submitted to life's treacheries and accepted its humiliating compromises. He would lodge itinerant circuses in his courtyard, elephants and all, in protest against the town's respectability, and ruin the once-flourishing family business in lawsuit upon disastrous lawsuit. A silent bond of hatred and contention had linked him to his wife and, after her death, to his daughter-in-law, in whose self-loathing he recognized his own inner state. Hardly ever moving out of the house which was a hateful prison to her, she would put on make-up for her solitude, and above all for the mirrors against which she tried to protect herself by means of drawn curtains and a discreet twilight. And the old man would walk every day to the Drowned Sailors' Wall and envy their death. At last death, that passionately loved foe, allowed him an end to his game when, in a final and most fitting gesture of unconscious rage, he accidentally split his skull with an axe.

Perken is cast in the same mold as the dead old man; he is approaching the fateful "age of defeat." The same suicidal

[19] *Ibid.*, p. 23.
[20] *Ibid.*, p. 29.

hatred convulses him and makes his own body above all, and the entire world around him, appear to him like an incarnation of suffering and defeat, an inescapable prison. What troubles him is not being killed, not death as such. What he finds unendurable is the thought of a death that is not chosen: the failing of his strength, the weakening of his power of assertion and domination. "Death, the real death, is a man's gradual decline . . . to feel shut up in a life there's no escaping, like a dog in its kennel!"[21] he exclaims bitterly while studying his face in the mirror. The most treacherous foe of all is the death lurking in his very limbs. At the end of *The Royal Way*, when he lies helpless, dying, consumed by fever and hatred, his glance falls on his hand, and he hates the semblance of life that is left in that mortal fragment of him:

> In his precipitate flight towards a world primeval as the forest, a hateful thought persisted in his mind: that hand of his, that white thing yonder, with its fingers higher than the heavy palm, its nails clawing the threads of the trouserseam, somehow recalled the spiders hooked to their webs in the warm leafage; like spiders dangling in the viscid undergrowth, it hung poised before his fascinated eyes, as he floundered through a world of formless things. And that hand was—death.[22]

More symbolically even than his healthy hand, his infected leg mirrors to Perken the inevitable process of destruction of which he is a victim. It symbolizes the screen that bars him from a forever-elusive eternity, the hopeless desire for which consumes him with rage.

21 *Ibid.*, p. 53.
22 *Ibid.*, p. 284.

To dominate this treacherous body, to conceal it from his own and the world's sight, Perken, like Garine, like all of the "conquerors," assumes a mask of impersonality, to shield him and make him immune. Yet, beneath this harness, no measure of alienation can prevail against the intolerable nakedness of the self. Unlike more mediocre or more raving "mythomaniacs"—this is what the captain of the ship calls Perken in discussing him with Claude—Perken is not deceived by his own legend. A frustrated but lucid pursuer of immortality, he has a deep and painful knowledge of the impossibility of silencing his demons or of severing himself from them. He speaks disdainfully of Mayrena, the ephemeral, heroic king of the Sedangs: "I see him as a player-king, bent on acting his own biography. You Frenchmen usually have a weakness for that sort of man, who prefers giving a fine performance to actual success."[23]

Perken knows that creating a mythical role for himself is but a poor sport if the myth fails to be effective; that is, if it does not transform the entire world into a mirror in which the self can see itself in turn transformed, so that it may at last accept itself and believe in its own reality. For the magic transmutation which Perken seeks to operate on the world, he seeks in truth to operate on the self alone. He does not care for the world, for other beings. Speaking of the grandiose adventure of his life, he says to Claude: "Looks as if I'd staked my life on a venture too big for me.—But that venture masked the rest of the world from me, and, on occasion, I've needed that pretty badly."[24] The dialectic within him, involving a deep sense of powerlessness and non-

23 *Ibid.*, p. 15.
24 *Ibid.*, pp. 92–93.

being, and a correspondingly burning need to assert at all costs the reality and the meaning of his existence, reaches such a dynamic pitch that nothing short of the whole world can be sufficient testimony to him of the self's reality. And so he flings out the veil of his legendary power far and wide, until it covers vast regions, among which are the territories of most of the free tribes of Siam, until he holds the alien world of men with his crystal-sharp intelligence and his machine guns, and the host of women who cross his path with his relentless erotic compulsion.

But gradually, inevitably, the veil is pierced, and reflections of his true state of despair and imprisonment begin to emerge. He recalls the time when his mistress Sarah began to hate him with a fierce intensity. From the day when she understood that her destiny was shaped by him, that he was the irrefutable limit of the prison which would forever exclude all her unfulfilled hopes and possibilities, the bond that linked her to him became for her an intolerable chain. "She began to loathe the sight of me as she loathed her mirror."[25] And as she ceased reflecting his mythic glory, he hated himself in her as he has henceforth hated himself in all women, in whose passive anonymous bodies he would seek in vain to find himself. In the midst of the stream of frantic sexual encounters, each of which spells to him another possibility of affirming the fugitive and doubted self, he finds himself exhausted, haunted by the dread of impotence.

At last every woman he has possessed, every will he has subdued, every thing he has ever accomplished, will lie dead before his eyes, like his own corpse.

25 *Ibid.*, p. 14.

As Perken consents to participate in Claude's expedition, fascinated by the young man's still undaunted courage and power which he hopes to fuse with his own waning strength, their glances meet in a mirror. It is an impersonal encounter of two destinies that recognize themselves in one another as "being penned in a private universe, as incommunicable as the blind man's or the lunatic's," a universe in which, in Claude's haunted mind, "the forests and its temples seemed gradually to come to monstrous life, malevolent as the great beasts of the jungle."[26] Nothing personal links the two men, nothing communicable; only that "which lies deepest in the heart of man . . . their common obsession with death."[27] It is this recognition of Perken as one who holds the key to the secret of his own life which in fact places Claude's fate under the star of Saturn, and draws him clearly into that chain of a common curse that links the Promethean rebels. Before they even arrive at their destination, he has a foreboding of the bitterest of servitudes:

> He might be killed, might disappear—it mattered little to him, for he had small interest in his own survival—yet, thus at least, he would have had the fight, if not the victory. But, living, to endure the vanity of life gnawing him like a cancer; all his life long to feel the sweat of death lie clammy on his palm . . . unbearable! Whence, indeed, if not from death, came his fierce desire, dense with the odor of death-ridden flesh, for all that is immortal?[28]

As their plans merge, Perken's participation in the search for the old Khmer sculptures transforms the expedition into a quest for power. For Perken, the expedition is the final

26 *Ibid.*, p. 58.
27 *Ibid.*, p. 53.
28 *Ibid.*, p. 56.

struggle for money (the statues command magnificent prices) with which he will purchase machine guns and bolster the faltering double game he plays with the French colonial government and the dissident tribes. In turn, Claude is drawn into the venture that has, above other things, brought Perken back to the Siamese forests: his search for Grabot, the disappeared rebel. The mysterious prison chain that has linked Claude to his grandfather, to Mayrena's legend, to Perken, now leads Perken to uncover, with Claude as witness, that ominous last link. They must both find Grabot in order to read in his face the prophecy it holds in store for them.

"Once again," says Berger at the end of *The Walnut Trees of Altenburg,* "Pascal comes back to my mind: Imagine a large number of men in chains, all condemned to death, every day some of them being butchered before the others' eyes, and in their fate those who remain see a reflection of their own condition. . . . This is the image of man's fate. . . . Perhaps anguish always wins out; perhaps the joy given to the only animal that knows it is not eternal is poisoned in its source." [29]

Whatever unconscious element of affirmation and hope there was in Claude's plan to retrieve some of the great art treasures from the jungle is shattered by the wave of anguish that rushes over the two heroes and the entire scene as the men, in following Grabot's traces, are drawn into a nightmare land of death that surpasses in terror even the jungle they have crossed. They proceed to the very heart of the dissident region and find themselves surrounded by the immobility and silence not only of nature at her darkest and

[29] André Malraux, *Les Noyers de l'Altenburg* (Paris: Gallimard, 1948), p. 289.

grimmest but of the half-savage and hostile Mois. A multiple, naked grimace of death stares at them:

> On the emptiness before the white men nothing stirred; time alone lived in it, meting out their fate. The passing minutes seemed immured within the ring-fence of those bestial faces, in which eternity was incarnate—an obdurate barrier that nothing happening in the outside world could cross, nothing could permeate. . . . They were like animals at bay, a horde of beasts of prey, the Mois watching them, biding their time to spring.[30]

Steadily, the confrontation becomes more unearthly, more demonic, as their eyes are fixed on that "sea of bestial faces . . . as little human, as implacable as the gaur's skull with its grinning death's-head teeth."[31]

The eyes of the Mois are all converging on a hut, barricading it, as it were, against the strangers. That hut harbors what they have come to find, and it turns out to be a very symbol of a jealous god's vengeful contrivance. In its pitch-black interior they discover a blind, dumb, filthy monster, a bell tinkling around his neck, tethered to a grindstone and turning slowly round and round—a slave: Grabot. On his unrecognizable face, all humanity is blotted out. The gesture of untying him is vain, as vain as the anguished questions they ask him to relieve their dread, to hear at least his voice, last vestige of a man's humanity. The voice that answers them is soundless, aloof, inhuman. It slowly articulates one word, "nothing," sealing the truth of what was once a man and is now a living cadaver. Hatred has devoured Grabot from within; it made him at one time deliberately destroy one of

30 *The Royal Way,* p. 199.
31 *Ibid.,* p. 204.

his eyes to have one of his officers whom he despised punished.

Fate has now finished Grabot from without through the savages whom he came to subdue. They have gouged out his remaining eye and tethered him to the millstone. An eye for an eye. The doom he embodies and foreshadows for the two men is so terrible to behold that Claude is tempted to shoot him, "if only for the satisfaction of wiping out that face of hate incarnate, and annihilating that reminder of his own human lot, as a murderer lops off his tell-tale finger."[32] From Grabot, Claude's eyes move to Perken whose features are petrified with dread at that moment. Then the anguish of total solitude grips him in the stomach like "the panic of a man left to his fate amongst a crowd of madmen ready to leap at him."[33] When Perken looks up in a state of delirium, he sees Grabot, head sunk on his chest, his face covered by his long hair, slowly shambling round and round the hut as if he were still harnessed to the millstone; he has returned to his servitude.

In *The Days of Wrath*, we find the civilized Western reflection of this "blind kingdom of fate": it is the concentration camp. Like the Asiatic jungle and the living specters that inhabit it, it is a realm of gloom, of silence and timeless horror. It too threatens to transform into blind madmen those whom it holds captive. Kassner, the solitary prisoner and hero of *The Days of Wrath*, discovers himself in an underworld in which all reality is lit up from below and takes on a grotesque and strange appearance. He sees his

32 *Ibid.,* p. 198.
33 *Ibid.,* p. 204.

torturers, the S. A. guards, who come into his cell to beat
him, "shapeless, with only their chins and cheekbones lit up
from below, surmounted by their squat shadows that were
flitting about on the ceiling like enormous spiders."[34] His
hole of a cell has an autonomous, suffocating life in which
the only reality is the crushing heaviness of the stone. The
thick walls seem alive, riddled as they are with cells in which
those of the prisoners who are still able to walk move about
like tireless centipedes. Kassner turns round and round in
the circular cell which offers no point on which to focus his
eye or attention; then, fearing to go mad, he lies down on
the floor, assuming instinctively the position of the dead,
feet together, hands crossed on his chest.

Kassner's position expresses the limitless servitude of man,
just as his turning about in the circle reflects the eternal
movement of the planets in their heavenly orbit. "The stars
would forever move in the same orbit in the stellar firma-
ments of fate, and forever too the planets would turn in the
immense universal prison, like the prisoners in their prison
yard, like himself in his dungeon."[35] All is engulfed in the
darkness, in the timeless time of prison, in a perpetual "forever," poisonous as a black spider.[36]

[34] André Malraux, *Le Temps du Mépris* (Paris: Gallimard, 1935), p. 42.
[35] *Ibid.*, p. 60.
[36] *Ibid.*, p. 61.

2

Carnival: Dance of Death

The black, timeless pit is one of the birthplaces of the imagination. Both on the level of concrete reality and as a metaphysical symbol, it not only constitutes the center of Malraux's works and of what he calls our "temps déshérité," but again and again Malraux reveals its summoning power, that stinging bite that activates all human faculties—mind, will, imagination—either toward the discovery of man's power of transcending his prisoner's estate, or toward his active and fateful collaboration in its destruction of him. Halfway between the multitude of the weak who succumb to suffering silently or with a whimper and who remain almost completely unseen and unheard in the early novels, and the heroes of the later works who transcend the closed prison cell of fate on the soaring wings of a true vision and strength, we find the "conquerors"—those strong in despair only. They seek to escape the darkness which presses in on them from without by covering it over, as it were, by the inner night, that demon of despair whose favorite guise is that of an angel of light, a luminous godhead. By consenting to become prisoners of their inner "monstre de rêve," they hope to sever the chains that bind

24

them to the world prison of spiritual, moral, and physical
defection. But no deliverance ensues; instead, a mysterious
wedding is consummated between the two faces of Saturn,
between the cosmic cycle of eternal recurrence—cruelly impervious to either divine or human intervention, and linking the prisoner's rounds in his universal prison cell to the
movement of the planets, and the "monstre de rêve," that
delirious "will to godhead"—chaotically claiming absolute
freedom and destroying the "quality of man" from within.

A strange illusion of light is created when, in the course
of its revolutions, the nocturnal aspect of a world apparently
forsaken by the light of divine providence and abandoned
to the power of Saturn hits upon and is reflected by the
saturnine or demonic pole of human consciousness, its counterpart. In the "conqueror" novels and in *Man's Fate*, in
which the "conquerors" play an important role, we have the
first act of the great drama evolving throughout Malraux's
work; namely man's dialogue with the evil star under whose
sign this century seems placed. The first act is a dance of
death. It is not a dialogue, but rather an ecstatic encounter
and fusion of the saturnine in man with the dark face of the
"planet" he inhabits—that is, our contemporary world of
wars and concentration camps.

In a succession of dazzling scenes, each of which bears
the character of a private apocalypse, Malraux depicts for us
those foredoomed "conquests" of the night which are but
surrenders in disguise. As in *Tales of Hoffman*, so in *Man's
Fate* the carnival stage is set by means of a phantom illumination that lights up a succession of masquerades, nocturnal
scenes outside time and reality, in which we see a host of
solitary figures, Europeans and a westernized Chinaman,

defiantly spin around themselves the magic circle of an absolute freedom. At the culmination of their frenzied rounds they will sink into the very night they have challenged, now darker and more impenetrable than before. But in the brief intoxicating moment that precedes, darkness becomes light and slavish frenzy assumes the appearance of total deliverance: in much the same manner as the Roman Saturnalia in which the slaves were given the illusion of being free and, what is more, of being served by their masters. Dread is transfigured by the imagination into ecstasy, and the world-prison becomes a carnival stage via the gambling roulette. The slave dancing with his cruel god assumes that god's mask, becomes one with him—fate doubly incarnate, a god.

Malraux renders this magic metamorphosis in the gambling scene by means of a profound symbol: the spinning ball that magnetizes the eyes of the Frenchman Clappique and the other gamblers amidst the noisy, frenzied night-life of Shanghai. It symbolizes all at once fate's all-devouring cycle which is as immutable within itself as it seems capricious to the victim which it crushes, the victim's march in his prison cell and, finally, the carnival dance into which he transforms his march in a state of willful delusion, seeing himself transfigured in its course into a sacrificial godhead. In a twilight state of consciousness in which despair and the will to madness re-enforce one another, Clappique stakes his own life and the life of Kyo, one of the Communist leaders of the Shanghai uprising, on this ball. The precious minutes in which he can still procure from Kyo the money he needs to leave China, and at the same time warn Kyo of his imminent arrest, tick by. Significantly, this fatal gambling

scene occurs the very eve of the day when the uprising will
be dealt its death blow: the Kuomintang has issued orders
for the arrest of the Communist leaders. Chiang Kai-shek's
police are already on their way to seize, torture, and execute
them. It is an apocalyptic night, in which the revolution
itself is seen dancing to the fatal tune of treachery and expediency, crushing in a deadly embrace all those men and
elements within it that might have brought about a true
victory—namely, a better life for the famished and diseased
multitudes of China.

Glued to his seat at the roulette table, Clappique assumes
the very role of his master, that fate which, in the form of
anxiety, has already undone him to the point of his appearing
to others like a man "who does not exist." Slowly but surely
losing, he tosses away everything he has left in an orgy of
liberation from time, from moral responsibility, from himself, from life.

> That ball which was slowing down was a destiny—*his*
> destiny. He was not struggling with a creature, but with
> a kind of god; and this god, at the same time, was him-
> self. . . . he had the feeling of seizing his life, of holding
> it suspended to the whim of that absurd ball. Thanks to
> it he was able for the first time to gratify at once the two
> Clappiques that composed him, the one who wanted to
> live and the one who wanted to be destroyed. Why look at
> the watch? He threw Kyo back into a world of dreams; it
> seemed to him that he was sustaining that ball, no longer
> with counters, but with his own life—by not meeting Kyo
> he lost all chance of getting any more money—and with
> the life of another; and the fact that the other was wholly
> unaware of it gave to the ball . . . the living reality of
> conjunctions of planets, of chronic diseases, of everything
> by which men believe their destinies to be governed. What

did that ball, hesitating on the edges of the compartments like a dog's muzzle, have to do with money? Through its agency he was embracing his own destiny—the only means he had ever found of possessing himself! To win, no longer in order to take flight, but to remain, to risk more, so that the stake of his conquered liberty would render the gesture even more absurd! Leaning on his forearm, no longer even looking at the ball which continued to roll, more and more slowly, the muscles of his calves and shoulders trembling, he was discovering the very meaning of gambling, the frenzy of losing.[37]

The all-absorbing game crowns his lifelong maneuvers to drown out the ever-increasing dread of the void, the anxiety of nonbeing, by removing him as far as possible from true being and into the orbit of the "evil spirit." He is all afire with the illusion of suddenly being a god, able to do anything he chooses, and at the same time he is lucidly aware that it is an illusion, that he is finally trapped in his own disguise of madness as a moth is caught by the light.

This "conjunction of planets," in which Clappique's inner despair encounters—as if by an inevitable, fateful necessity —all that would join it from without in its drive to annihilate him, is rendered persistently by Malraux through many and recurring closed circular images and movements. There is not only the spinning ball, but the roulette, revolving planets, the moth imprisoned within the orbit of the light; and finally, the ironic "halo" which surrounds Clappique's Punchinello-like figure and blots out his face: "The Baron's face was scarcely visible; the large illuminated cat, the sign-board of the *Black Cat,* surrounded him like a

[37] André Malraux, *Man's Fate,* trans. Haakon M. Chevalier (The Modern Library edn.; New York: Random House, 1934), pp. 257-58.

halo."[38] There is much of Nietzsche's concept of eternal recurrence in this fateful turning of the "conqueror's" destiny
within and around the orbit of Saturn, culminating in his
"dance of death," that dizzying round which he dances with
fate as his chosen bride. Traces of it persist in as late a work
as *The Voices of Silence:* "The eternal flux on whose mysterious rhythm we are borne ineluctably, in a never ceasing
drift of stars. Apollo, Prometheus—or Saturn; Aphrodite or
Ishtar; a resurrection of the flesh or the Dance of Death."[39]

We see Clappique will this conjunction, deliberately do
his share in manipulating reality around him so as to bring
it about. In his hope of finding liberation from dread in thus
abandoning himself, or rather, wedding himself to Saturn's
evil presence in the world (to the point where the two become indistinguishable from one another), there is something of the conjurer's exorcising magic.

To exorcise dread by this kind of "blood wedding" is a
violent way of denying its reality. Despite Clappique's anger
at hearing the painter, Kama, serenely denying suffering at
a moment when his own anguish seems uncontrollable, the
apocalypse of the gambling scene bears out his inability to
face the undisguised reality of dread, and his subsequent
need to assume the traits of the very divinity that destroys
him and to play its role. It is no wonder, as Malraux has
pointed out in *The Voices of Silence,* that the West has,
since the nineteen twenties, been fascinated by the masks of
Polynesia and the New Hebrides and by primitive fetishes.

[38] *Ibid.,* p. 36. This last one is a curious image; it makes one think of a
passage in *Saturne* in which Malraux says of Goya: "His imagination lights
up in the dark like a cat's eyes."
[39] "The Creative Process," trans. Stuart Gilbert (Garden City: Doubleday,
1953), p. 323.

Do they not bear an affinity to our own "carnival," "in which man is dispossessed of his prerogative in favor of the denizens of some phantasmagoric pageant of the powers of darkness."[40] Those masks too were born of dread and they had a magical function: to conjure the demonic and thereby liberate man from its power. Unlike the art of the West, Romanesque sculpture, for example, which likewise claims much of our attention today, and which responds to dread and suffering with faith—that is, affirmation of a positive order and of meaning—these masks express a saturnine, an essentially negative, vision of the world and of man's place in it.

In the mask of the "conqueror," we see essentially the same defiance, the same rebellion. Assimilating the features of Saturn is the answer of the God-obsessed and forsaken rebel to man's finite and death-bound estate, which involves a defiance so bitter and yet so ecstatic that death alone can crown it. The mask is designed to deny the self and to transmute him who wears it in turn into a punishing god-head, thus delivering him from punishment. Herein lies the true essence of carnival: "The joining of death, gambling and the nocturnal part of the world."[41]

Like Clappique, the terrorist Ch'en is seen as a "murderous insect," as "a moth who secretes his own light—in which he will destroy himself."[42] In his self-inflicted, violent death the wedding of inner and outer darkness is actually consummated in blood.

In the first scene of *Man's Fate,* a "dim, motionless light" hovers over the lonely hotel room in which Ch'en has just

[40] "Aftermath of the Absolute," *The Voices of Silence,* p. 575.
[41] *Saturne,* p. 172.
[42] *Man's Fate,* p. 166.

committed his first murder and which he has by this act transformed into a no-man's land of immemorial sacrifice. Ch'en is paralyzed by a dread at once horrible and solemn: "he was alone with death, alone in a place without men, limply crushed by horror and by the taste of blood."[43] When he steps out on the balcony, his dread is answered in a way which frightens him, by the "poignant serenity" of the sky and of the stars "resuming their endless course," by the vast expanse of darkness "like the invisible sea in the distance."[44] He leaves the hotel and, having crossed the city whose lights remind him of the millions of living men from whom he now feels cut off forever, he reaches with relief the darkness of the city limits:

> Here nothing remained of the world but night, to which Ch'en instinctively attuned himself as to a sudden friend-ship: this nocturnal, anxious world was not opposed to murder. A world from which men had disappeared, a world without end; would daylight ever return upon those crumbling tiles, upon all those narrow streets, at the end of which a lantern lighted a windowless wall . . . ?[45]

To Ch'en in whom a sorrowful adolescence and the teach-ing of a Calvinist have awakened a passionate awareness of the supernatural, human existence cut off by sin from limit-less love is limitless terror. Unredeemed by grace, it is worse than a torment; it is a fatality so inhuman that he feels him-self a stranger to it, unbound by its laws. He appoints him-self to avenge his outraged purity in a murder that is to be simultaneously a self-immolation and the hate-saturated and

43 *Ibid.*, p. 12.
44 *Ibid.*, p. 13.
45 *Ibid.*, p. 16.

frenzied conquest of the "stellar night of the Mothers."

As the Shanghai insurrection approaches its climax, Ch'en decides to kill Chiang Kai-shek. In the room where he announces his decision, the light turns livid as before a storm. "In the diffused half-light the bellies of the storm lamps glowed with a curious effect—rows of inverted question marks."[46] In a symbolic accident, he stumbles over one of the lamps; it falls and breaks with a tinkle. His shadow looms large above the heads of the two young Chinese to whom he expounds the terrorist's mystic cult of murder.

As he abandons himself to the idea of his solitary "conquest," he feels himself advancing into a region where all human reality ceases to exist; place and time cease to matter and the destinies around him, even those of his companions, recede, become unsubstantial, then intolerable. "He no longer belonged to China . . . a complete liberty gave him over completely to his mind."[47]

> The only thing which his present state of mind did not transform into nothingness was the idea of creating those doomed Executioners, that race of avengers. This birth was taking place in him, like all births, with agony and exaltation—he was not master of it. He could no longer endure any presence.[48]

Feeling completely alone, cut off even from his fellow-terrorists, and confirmed in his mission by his intense hatred and by the rapture that begins to envelop him—that "thick, deep ecstasy toward—downward"[49]—Ch'en prepares to throw

[46] *Ibid.*, p. 194.
[47] *Ibid.*, p. 64.
[48] *Ibid.*, p. 197.
[49] *Ibid.*, p. 158.

a bomb under Chiang Kai-shek's car. Blowing up together with it, he will, like Clappique, surrender "to the moment that would join him to himself in a dizzy embrace."[50]

The desolate night of the China of rice-fields and marshes had reached the almost deserted avenue. Dim in the mist, the lights that passed between the slits of the partly open shutters, went out one by one; the last reflections clung to the wet rails, to the telegraph insulators; they gradually grew fainter; soon Ch'en could see them only on the vertical sign-boards covered with gilt characters. This misty night was his last night, and he was satisfied. He would blow up with the machine, in a blinding flash that would illuminate this hideous avenue for a second and cover a wall with a sheaf of blood. [Suddenly the general's car emerges out of the darkness.] He ran towards it with ecstatic joy, threw himself upon it with his eyes shut.[51]

Time is annulled in this spectacular moment in which the primordial night is revealed and deepened in terror's fervent embrace.[52] Paradoxically, Ch'en in the moment that precedes his death, Clappique at the roulette, Perken facing the Mois, experience their orgiastic descent into the private subterranean palace of dreams and obsessions as a culmination of deliverance. What seems to them the assertion of an absolute freedom is in fact the total consent of the fatalist to being imprisoned in the closed cycle of eternal recurrence. Once trapped in this cycle and its fatal reversibility of meaning and values, the "conqueror's" triumph of power over fate actually is his joining himself to it in deathly self-oblit-

[50] *Ibid*. Cf. Perken's same experience of fascination and horror as he walks toward the Mois, expecting to die at their hand.

[51] *Ibid.*, pp. 247-48.

[52] Cf. Rachel Bespaloff's impressive analysis of Malraux's rebels in "Notes sur André Malraux," *Cheminements et Carrefours* (Paris: Vrin, 1938).

eration. He is crushed between eternity and the moment, between his all-consuming quest for an absolute, be it a god of destruction if not a god of love, and the primordial chaos within him as they fuse, with no human reality or time interceding and saving him within its limits.

Malraux's solitary metaphysical rebels remind us indeed of Nietzsche who, in anguish, proclaimed the "death of God" and later, in his madness, saw himself as the crucified god Dionysos. In his Postface to *The Conquerors,* written in 1949, Malraux sums up the effect of this despairing separation from the divine, and the ensuing romantic mock marriage with the demonic: "Le drame actuel de l'Europe, c'est la mort de l'homme."[53] As in Garine's Christmas carnival, so Malraux's "conquerors," in the disguise of their vengeful master, arrogating to themselves his freedom and omnipotence, toss to the stake the "black figures of the gods." Yet no new god is born. "I would have liked to see the dawn,"[54] says Garine, but the mock holocaust does not transform the "priests" into gods; no new star rises for them. Instead, as Malraux shows us, after the mock murder of the gods in the carnival, or upon the dance of death in which the anguished wooer of Saturn immolates himself, follows a dance of death in which he will immolate others. The gruesome analogy and consequence of that carnival scene is the real scene of execution remembered by Katov—one of the heroes of the uprising in *Man's Fate*—who was among the condemned but survived the ordeal; the black statues are embodied there in "those pale shadows on the greenish snow at dawn, trans-

[53] *Les Conquérants,* Version définitive, Postface 1949 (Paris: Grasset, 1949), p. 259.
[54] *Ibid.,* p. 171.

parent, shaken by convulsive sneezes in the face of the machine-guns."[55] In human history the masks are always wrenched away in the end; and when the false dawn terminates the masquerade "c'est la fin de l'ironie, l'accent de l'incurable nuit,"[56] the death of man.

After a lifelong game of dissimulation and masquerading, of heeding the inner, irrational demons at the expense of his conscience, his dignity, an inherent sense of being and relation, a situation which is climaxed in the gambling scene, Clappique discovers with horror that he has succeeded in destroying himself. His madness, so long controlled by him, has gotten control of him. He has lost his identity. Having seemingly managed to escape the common lot of man— family, work, all kinds of bonds—he is condemned to watch spellbound as fear rises and overflows the immense vacuum that he has so carefully created within himself and that turns him into a terrified madman. Too paralyzed by dread, too deeply sunk in the void to commit suicide, he heaps contempt on his image in the mirror and forces it, docile mask, to reflect for him in full his degradation:

> . . . "You don't want to die. You don't want to die, you little bastard! And yet look at yourself—a fine face to use for a dead man . . ."
> He drew still nearer, his nose almost touching the glass; he twisted his face, mouth open, into a gargoyle's grimace, and as if the mask had answered him:
> "Everyone can't be dead? Obviously: it takes a little of everything to make a world. Pshaw! When you're dead you'll go to Paradise. And what a companion God will be for a fellow of your sort . . ."

55 *Man's Fate*, p. 76.
56 *Saturne*, p. 64.

He made a different face, mouth shut and drawn towards the chin, eyes half-opened, like a carnival samurai. And immediately, as if he had found a way of expressing directly in all its intensity the torment which words were not adequate to translate, he began to make faces, transforming himself into a monkey, an idiot, a terrified person, an apoplectic, into all the grotesques that a human face can express. This no longer sufficed: he used his fingers, drawing out the corners of his eyes, enlarging his mouth for the toad face of the man-who-laughs, flattening his nose, pulling out his ears. Each of these faces spoke to him, revealed to him a part of himself hidden by life; this debauchery of the grotesque in the solitary room, with the night mist piled against the window, was assuming the atrocious and terrifying humor of madness. He heard his own laughter—a single note, the same as his mother's; and, suddenly perceiving his face, he withdrew with horror and sat down, panting.[57]

This metamorphosis achieved by dread and its phantasmagoria is but the expansion and deepening of night to an opaqueness which no glimmer of light can penetrate. It has transformed a man into a hollow shell, in which terror's anonymous monologue is heard echoing the immemorial voice of death.

The same illusion of liberation from dread through ultimate dread and the fatal metamorphosis it produces in its victim is seen also in the case of the shopkeeper Hemmelrich. Hemmelrich is not an intellectual and he differs from Clappique and Ch'en in that his rebellion is confined to the instinctual level; unlike them, he is a pure victim of the world's absurdity and injustice with no part of him remaining aloof as spectator to reflect upon his situation. Yet, on

[57] *Man's Fate,* pp. 275–76.

a more primitive plane, Malraux reveals in him the same saturnalian illumination and mock transmutation from slave to master. Hemmelrich has been kept back from participating in the uprising because he has felt morally compelled to stay with his wife and sick child. Shame and self-contempt have nearly driven him out of his mind while he has stood by and watched his companions risk their lives. There is heavy street-fighting and when he returns to his shop he finds his wife's and child's tortured dead bodies.

> In spite of the catastrophe, of the sensation of having the ground give way under his feet, leaving nothing but empty space, he could not banish from his mind the atrocious, weighty, profound joy of liberation. With horror and satisfaction he felt it rumble within him like a subterranean river, grow nearer. The corpses were there, his feet which were stuck to the floor were glued by their blood, nothing could be more of a mockery than these murders—especially that of the sick child: he seemed even more innocent than the dead woman;—but now he was no longer impotent. Now, *he too could kill.* It came to him suddenly that life was not the only mode of contact between human beings, that it was not even the best; that he could know them, love them, possess them more completely in vengeance than in life. Again he became aware of his shoe-soles, stuck to the floor, and tottered: muscles were not aided by thought. But an intense exultation was overwhelming him, the most powerful that he had ever known; he abandoned himself to this frightful intoxication with entire consent.[58]

On the run, he joins his communist comrades at the post which is being machine-gunned by Chiang Kai-shek's men and is filled with the stench of death and the screams of the wounded.

[58] *Ibid.,* pp. 270-71.

Himself wounded, he manages to creep out of the building
in the back where everything is deserted when, suddenly, "a
shadow appeared" behind the barbed wire—an enemy.

The monster-man, bear and spider combined—continued to disentangle itself from the wires. Alongside of the
black mass a line of light marked the ridge of his large
pistol. Hemmelrich felt himself at the bottom of a hole,
fascinated less by the creature that was moving so slowly,
approaching like death itself, than by everything that
followed it, everything that was once more going to crush
him, like a coffin-lid screwed down over a living person;
it was everything that had chocked his every-day life, which
was now returning to crush him with one blow. . . .
everything mingled in a haze of thirst, of fever and of
hatred.[59]

As the man—anonymous embodiment of fate—draws nearer,
Hemmelrich leaps on him and in the ensuing interlocking
of bodies, kills him with savage force, then puts on his dead
adversary's dress, an officer's uniform. Thus disguised, he
dupes those who would kill him and succeeds in getting away
from the holocaust at the post.

Like Clappique, he survives the carnival, but only in the
flesh. What is left of him is no longer a man but rather a
grim incarnation of hatred capable of but one significant
gesture—killing. The man in him is dead and he is a monster, a creature able to live only through destruction. He is
bound now to that ominous clan of executioners who reign
over prisons and concentration camps and who, from König,
chief of Chiang Kai-shek's police, down to the warder that
whips a lunatic prisoner in a gruesome scene, perpetuate the
murder of their own humanity by torturing others and chang-

59 *Ibid.*, pp. 291–92.

ing them in turn into beasts. The deadly transformation has reduced Hemmelrich's being to that dark, chaotic part within himself of which, through a peculiar light-effect, one of the first scenes in *Man's Fate* had already given us a glimpse and a premonition. In that scene he is seen standing under a vertical ray of light. The light, replacing his deep-set eyes by "two black stains"—those black stains so essential in Goya's etchings and also in modern painting—transforms him into a lugubrious specter of hatred.

When Clappique talks to König to plead for Kyo's life which only a few hours ago he held in his hands and gambled away, and hears König refuse and expound to him his henchman's creed, he suddenly grasps the hitherto mysterious relation between himself and all those solitary avengers. Listening to König,

> he remained dazed by that complete intoxication, which only blood could satisfy: he had seen enough wrecks from the civil wars of China and Siberia to know that a deep humiliation calls for a violent negation of the world; only drugs, neuroses, and blood insistently shed, can feed such solitudes. He understood now why König had liked his company, as he was not unaware that in his presence all reality vanished.[60]

The treacherous power of the Saturnalia to transform its maskers into corpses or beasts extends also over the place which serves as the stage. Symbolically, as Chiang Kai-shek prepares to defeat the uprising by stabbing the Communists in the back, the light over Hankow, supposed backbone of the uprising, assumes a false, trancelike serenity. Ushering in the holocaust of Shanghai, the light over Hankow is seen

[60] *Ibid.*, p. 285.

blending "far, far up with the serenity of the night," abandoning the city to all the crafts of magic: only "doctors . . .
casters of spells, astrologers and fortune-tellers continued
their timeless trades by the dim light that blotted out the
blood stains."[61] To the initiated eye of Kyo, one of the leaders of the uprising, Hankow reveals itself to be, not what the
people have believed it to be, but a mere stage on which the
puppets of the fateful revolutionary machine are already
dancing to the tune of expediency and deceit.

In the Shanghai apocalypse, the Blue "conquerors" of the
city and Saturn join hands and all human reality is crushed
in their grip. In the prison, now filled with the newly arrested leaders, Kyo reflects upon the warder's brutality:

> . . . so true to the legend, the warder's vileness did not
> seem to him altogether real; and at the same time, it
> seemed to him a foul fatality, as if power were enough to
> change almost every man into a beast. Those obscure be-
> ings who stirred behind the bars, disturbing like the
> colossal insects and crustaceans in his childhood dreams,
> were no more human.[62]

[61] *Ibid.*, p. 142.
[62] *Ibid.*, p. 300.

3

Irremediable Doom

In what may be the last major surge of French romanticism in the tradition of the *poètes maudits*, Malraux sends his "masks"—his rebels in disguise—pirouetting down a "Styx bourbeux et plombé." There human reality is engulfed not only in the downward whirl of fate or gravity inherent in a deathbound universe that seems to bear no relation to a divine creator, but at the same time by that "monstre de rêves" which each one of his characters bears within himself. It in turn destroys its man, inevitably, from the moment he grants it kingship over himself and begins to make sacrifices to its majesty.

How much Garine, Perken, Claude, and the others have inherited from the *poètes maudits!* how much of that sense of estrangement, rebellion, and damnation that Gérard de Nerval evoked so powerfully in the *Chimères,* particularly in "El Desdichado."[63] Malraux's "conquerors" too belong to the race of the forsaken and accursed. They differ from their

---

[63] Cf. the first quatrain:
> Je suis le ténébreux, le veuf, l'inconsolé,
> Le Prince d'Aquitaine à la tour abolie.
> Ma seule *étoile* est morte,—et mon luth constellé
> Porte le *soleil* noir de la mélancolie.

nineteenth-century ancestors in that their *étoile* is no longer an ideal image to be pursued in dream visions, as Gérard pursued his Aurélia; their *étoile* is not an image but an idea: it is the will to self-deification, and they seek to project and translate this idea into concrete action. They have a sense of history and of events that was lacking in the *poètes maudits*.[64] Yet their drama is the same; namely that of an inner *dédoublement*, which seeks an outer stage on which to unfold and resolve itself.

Torn between the two extremes of boundless exaltation and boundless despair, the "conquerors" hope that in shifting this inner drama onto a scene of action, they may open up a way toward resolving it. Does not Garine hope that the success of his function will prevail over his anguish and silence it? But this hope is deluded. For that unresolved conflict within him in which actor and spectator, demiurge and victim, war against each other—the former staking all on power, the latter knowing that no power can prevail against the inevitable final defeat—is reflected on the outer stage in man's everlasting struggle to build an abiding city against the deadly powers of gravity and decomposition. Instead then of saving himself through exterior reality, Malraux's "conqueror" is, as it were, doubly condemned. He is pulled down in a spiral descent. Its course leads him from the initial impetus of inner anguish through the vicissitudes and failures of fighting Saturn "in the world," back into the deeper pit of a final estrangement from both the world and himself —to a death which is not only the end of life but the end of hope, "l'incurable nuit."

[64] Baudelaire's part in the revolution of 1848, when compared to the political action of Malraux's figures and even more to that of Malraux himself, merely proves this point.

As Malraux points out in *The Voices of Silence*, the sense of the "irremediable," which to him means the sense of man's fall and servitude both in the realm of nature and the realm of the sacred, has not in itself been confined to one particular period of human history, nor to one particular expression. It has not even been confined to periods of doubt or unbelief. In great periods of faith, the *trecento* for example, this very sense of the irremediable only deepened the believer's attitude of supplication and submission and his belief in an ultimate reconciliation through the mediating Christ. Giotto's "Nativity" expresses this attitude perfectly. Then, in the Renaissance, a very different vision, compounded of doubts and a new heroic sense of man's power and will to autonomy, gave birth to works like Michelangelo's "Night" or "Last Judgment," in which, in Malraux's description, "Christ is not a vanquisher of dragons but of men; men likewise of heroic stature by reason of their damnation, a surging mass of Promethean rebels, suffering but unsubdued."[65]

Still, man's relation to the divine remained essentially one of affirmation. From the Renaissance on, the sense of discord, of an irremediable, final separation, has grown steadily and with it the attitude of rebellion and despair. Goya's "Saturn," Baudelaire's "l'Irrémédiable" or "Le Goût du Néant" or any number of his sonnets, or Gérard's *Chimères* express an obsession with everything that reveals the deep chasm between creature and creator, between the demoniac incarnate in human existence and the lost and unknown ideal. Possessed alternately by dread and by their ideal, dispossessed of every power or form of mediation in a broken and hostile world, the heirs of this tradition seek in their turn by their power

[65] "The Creative Process," *The Voices of Silence*, p. 330.

of incantation to transmute their hell into a heaven, their despair into a private apocalypse; and in their "ecstasy toward downward" they sink to the bottom of Baudelaire's burning polar ice of damnation.

Within sight of one of the Moi fetishes—a woman weeping for the dead—Perken, whose life "was now rushing down a precipice," proudly exclaims: "Anyhow, there is something satisfactory in the mere thought that life is being annihilated." [66] He is seized by "a bitter joy, emptied of every hope, like wave-worn jetsam drawn up from the sea-depths deep as the dark night around them." [67] More deeply and deliberately entrenched in concrete reality than any romantic hero, because he has through his lifetime staked his fate on action and its success, Perken refuses, or is unable, to rise beyond the "absurd" limits of his concrete existence through a flight of the imagination, and he bitterly concedes defeat. He survives his fleetingly ecstatic surrender to nothingness long enough to state what constitutes for himself and indeed for his entire generation of "conquerors" the irremediable absurdity: that in his disinherited time not even death seems real; there is only the "I," surrounded by an immense void, and this "I" is doomed to disappear without leaving so much as a trace or a scar on the map of the world. "On the little nucleus of hope that was his life the world would set its stranglehold . . . and nothing in the universe could ever compensate him for his past and present sufferings: to be a living man was even more absurd than dying!" [68] "There is . . . no death. There's only . . . I . . . I who . . . am dying." [69]

[66] *The Royal Way,* p. 169.
[67] *Ibid.*
[68] *Ibid.,* pp. 282–83.
[69] *Ibid.,* p. 290.

Like a faltering tightrope dancer, the superman magician, his private myth failing him with the approach of death, crashes into the void. This void is always rendered by Malraux as dazzling light: the blazing sun in *The Royal Way,* or the headlights of the car into which Ch'en hurls himself with his bomb in *Man's Fate.* The "halo" surrounding and isolating the "conquerors," this light secreted by the "moths," blazes forth in the apocalyptic moment, then is blacked out. Ch'en has a premonition of this—his own fate —when he cries out at one moment: "Is even blood futile?"[70] After the apocalypse, complete darkness covers the scene in more than one sense. By means of it Malraux signifies to us the "incurable nuit" which descends after the "death of man," or rather, after the death of the "conqueror" or man-god. This death, so absurdly void of any impact, is the central event in the "age of assassins," prophesied by Rimbaud in the last century and realized in the present one. In its wake the only, the fundamental, value that was still left is seen hopelessly debauched; the only still unsuspect challenger of death, so simply named by Malraux "the quality of man," is shattered.

The germ of this debauchery is contained in the action itself of the "conquerors," no matter how visibly their action may bear the stamp of high seriousness, even of total self-sacrifice as in the case of Ch'en or Garine. For it never expresses a true dedication to a cause involving the subordination of the individual imagination and will to power and glory. On the contrary, the "conqueror's" action expresses his dedication to his innermost "monstre de rêves," to his chimera which seizes upon the outer "occasion" and inevita-

[70] *Man's Fate,* p. 109.

bly violates it by manipulating it for its own purpose. To
Ch'en it matters little whether he kills Chiang Kai-shek or
another. The identity of the victim is almost incidental. It
is immaterial to Garine that he is fighting for the people of
China; they are distasteful to him; if he adopts their cause
instead of some other, it is because fight he must and they
furnish the occasion.

Similarly Perken sets out with Claude in a quest for statues, not for love of their wondrous and unique beauty
but because the statues spell money, that most anonymous
and interchangeable token of power. The "conqueror's" violation of the world is seen most symbolically in Perken's and
Ferral's persistent need to rape, that is, to destroy the unique,
distinct, personal quality of human beings and to reduce
them to faceless, voiceless, dumb matter. Action then, for
the "conquerors," equates itself almost perforce with violation, violation first of "other" beings and then, inevitably,
through those "others," of the self.

> Never, it reverberates through Perken's mind as, near
> death already, he bends over the strange body of the
> prostitute, never would he apprehend, never share this
> woman's sensations; never could the frenzy which thrilled
> her body be for him anything but a proof of the unbridge-
> able gulf between them. Without love there can be no
> possession . . . he too closed his eyes, thrown back upon
> himself as on a noxious drug, drunk with a wild desire vio-
> lently to crush out of existence this stranger's face that
> urged him on to death.[71]

Clappique goes one step further and even refuses to take
seriously those "occasions" that seemingly dictate the acts of

[71] *The Royal Way*, pp. 249–50.

the others—revolutionary politics, finance, terrorism, "love."
All the "conquerors" are gamblers; he is the only overt one.
He incarnates most purely that debauchery which Malraux
refers to in *The Voices of Silence*, when he speaks of "modern barbarism" and defines it as being no longer "the rejection of the status of citizen" but beyond that "the rejection
of the estate of Man."[72]

The systematic *dérèglement* of exterior reality so as to
bring it into conformity with the "conqueror's" will is
crowned by Clappique's conscious *dérèglement* of his own
mind and, beyond that, of his very identity—to the point
where both are lost. With this figure, Malraux adds an image
of his own to Goya's "The Sleep of Reason Produces Monsters." Clappique, having sided with his demon of destructive
despair against all that is human in him—his many human
traits are now only gratuitous vestiges and merely accentuate
his monstrosity—is transformed by his own game into a mere
semblance of a man, *disponible,* ready to assume all masks,
to engage in all exploits with the terrible freedom of the
mad and the damned. Nothing any longer sets off the outer
from the inner reality, for reality is no more; the world is
but a phantom stage inhabited by indistinguishable specters
echoing his monologue. Having no passport, no money,
threatened with arrest if he remains in Shanghai, he saves
his skin by boarding one of the last ships to leave Shanghai,
disguised as a sailor. Like an evil epiphany, this scene marks
the false dawn that ends the Saturnalia: "He had found,
suddenly, by accident, the most dazzling success of his life.
No, men do not exist, since a costume is enough to escape
from oneself, to find another life in the life of others. . . .

[72] "Aftermath of the Absolute," p. 607.

Now I am living a story, not merely telling one!"[73] The most mythomaniac individual has by the end of the carnival become Everyman in the degraded sense of no man, a hollow man of "cavernous voice," an anonymous automaton of exchangeable parts.

The triumph of Saturn over the "conqueror," the latter's identification with and immolation to the evil divinity, need not then necessarily take the form of a bloody sacrifice. Most of Malraux's conquerors do indeed suffer a violent end. But there are also those whose humanity dissolves in a gentle, almost imperceptible descent, who sink into a pale limbo where a soft, diffuse light reduces everything to the same level of meaninglessness or unimportance. In this inhuman world, moral values cease to matter, emotions recede and become nebulous—it is a timeless realm of sensation and dream, as far removed from the moment and its contingencies as it is from joy or grief. Such is the world of the opium addict Gisors.

Unlike Clappique who has willfully gambled away his soul and mind, Gisors, through the habit of opium, has allowed his splendid and distinguished mind imperceptibly to drift off on its own, to separate itself from him and from the world, to become a pure spectator. When we first encounter Gisors, we watch his mind beholding reality through that light veil of alienation which filters all events, all beings, all emotions, his own and those of others, and admits them thus filtered into an artificial paradise of pure contemplation.

Contrasting sharply with Clappique the buffoon, Gisors, the French scholar, has assumed the mask of an Oriental sage. But for him too the world no longer actually exists. Just as

[73] *Man's Fate*, p. 313.

for the gambler it has become a kind of circus in which to
play the clown, so for the sage it has become a mere reflection,
in myriad phenomena, of the eternal life of the cosmos. With
gentle, aloof scorn Gisors meditates upon things and takes
comfort in their unreality. Only one thing, rather one being,
is real to him—Kyo, his son. Kyo is his counterpart and,
obscurely, his ideal. He is what Gisors himself has lacked the
courage to be: a man, one who has accepted the anguish of
existence without disguise, in whom contemplation has called
forth no withdrawal, but action; a tragic hero who is staking
his life on the realization of a meaning. Kyo is the justification of Gisors' life. As long as Kyo lives, the father remains
bound to the human world by at least this one living bond of
flesh and spirit. This single bond, this presence, suffices to
dominate the demons that the old man feels stirring within
him underneath the artificial serenity induced by the drug.
For even opium does not long remain all-powerful against
the dynamism of the human spirit, against the anguish to
which it is prey.

But even Kyo's presence begins to recede and to become
powerless to check Gisors' ever progressing flight from reality
under the stress of events. When Ch'en comes to confide to
Gisors, his former teacher, the first murder he has committed,
Gisors experiences a revulsion against this young pupil, and
a feeling of incongruity, as if his own Marxist teaching, his
clear and limpid thought, could not possibly have caused
this violent moral upheaval, that vulgar bloodshed. As he
muses over his helpless indifference to Ch'en's distress, his
thoughts seek refuge in his son Kyo. "If Kyo were to enter
and tell me, like Ch'en a little while ago: 'It is I who killed
Tang Yan Ta,' I would think, 'I knew it.' All the possibili-

ties within him echo in me with such force that whatever he might tell me, I would think, 'I knew it . . . .' " Through the window he looks out at the motionless and indifferent night, deeply disturbed suddenly by the thought that his son may be in grave danger without himself doing anything to help him. "But if I really knew it, and not in this uncertain and appalling fashion, I would save him. A painful affirmation of which he did not believe a word. What confidence did he have in his own mind?"[74]

An obsessive sense of his state of non-being, of hopeless remoteness from the teeming, throbbing drama of the revolution of which he is a witness, takes hold of him, now separating him even from his son. He wearily drops Kyo's photograph which he has taken out from under the opium tray and lights a pipe—his ever renewed and more and more final gesture of abdication. Slowly he sinks into a silent despair, which the opium fails this time to resolve completely.

> Two pipes. Formerly as soon as his craving began to be quenched, he would contemplate men with benevolence, and the world as an infinity of possibilities. Now in his innermost being, the possibilites found no place: he was sixty, and his memories were full of tombs. His exquisitely pure sense of Chinese art, of those bluish paintings on which his lamp cast only a dim light, of the whole civilization of suggestion which China spread around him, which, thirty years earlier, he had been able to put to such delicate uses—his sense of happiness—was now nothing more than a thin cover beneath which anguish and the obsession of death were awakening, like restless dogs stirring at the end of their sleep.[75]

74 *Ibid.*, pp. 70–71.
75 *Ibid.*, p. 72.

Despairing of ever being able to restore the bridges between himself and the world which he has, first unknowingly,
then out of a growing necessity, destroyed—by seeking refuge
from anxiety in opium and in his "subterranean imagination"—he now wills his isolation, even from his son. He
consciously chooses to leave behind Kyo and the world of
beings and events, and to entomb himself in that inner,
magic no-man's land of shadows—to find in it confirmation
of the world's unreality. "He felt himself penetrating into
a domain which belonged to him more than any other. With
his intruding consciousness he was anxiously treading a for-
bidden solitude where no one would ever join him."[76] Malraux accentuates the movement of descent by a further dim-
ming of the scene. The semidarkness becomes almost total
darkness as Gisors pushes back the lamp by a fraction of an
inch. We are plunged with him into a euphoric vision of a
silently decaying, crumbling world; it is fashioned out of a
memory; it is a scene of oriental stillness pervaded by delicate fragrances; these are the last faint echoes of a universe
inhabited by men. Then this vision, too, slowly melts away
and is absorbed in an infinite sense of absence:

> Forms, memories, ideas, all plunged slowly toward a
> liberated universe. He remembered a September afternoon
> when the solid gray of the sky made a lake's surface milky,
> in the meshes of vast fields of water-lilies; from the moldy
> gables of an abandoned pavilion to the magnificent and
> desolate horizon he saw only a world suffused with a
> solemn melancholy. Near his idle bell, a Buddhist priest
> leaned on the balustrade of the pavilion, abandoning his
> sanctuary to the dust, to the fragrance of burning aromatic
> woods; peasants gathering water-lily seeds passed by in a

[76] *Ibid.*, p. 73.

boat without the slightest sound; at the edge of the farthest flowers two long waves grew from the rudder, melted listlessly in the gray water. They were vanishing now in himself, gathering in their fan the oppressiveness of the world, but an oppressiveness without bitterness, brought by opium to an ultimate purity. His eyes shut, carried by great motionless wings, Gisors contemplated his solitude: a desolation that joined the divine, while at the same time the wave of serenity that gently covered the depths of death widened to infinity.[77]

There is no transformation of grief into a deeper, tragic awareness. What we witness is the opposite process: that fateful process of dissolution described before the time of Malraux by the romantics, best of all perhaps by Baudelaire in the second "Poème du Haschich." The ecstasy that accompanies Gisors' flight downward, as he leaves behind all weight, all forms, all discernible actuality, dissolves in its turn as he completes the illusory movement toward infinity. At the end of this descent, what has appeared to the liberated senses as a summit reveals itself as the bottom of an abyss. What has seemed to the mind total liberation is perceived by it now as the total loss of all vital tension, distinction, and meaning. This epiphany of death is essentially analogous to the moment of Perken's death, or Ch'en's, and to that final, irremediable obliteration of self at the end of Clappique's peregrinations.

But an awakening is still in store for Gisors, is inevitable in fact, as on the one hand the dope-induced infinity fades away and, in its turn, his concern for his son's safety summons him sharply. Is he still able to spring back from the precipice and reject its tempting call to an artificial paradise

[77] *Ibid.*, p. 74.

of oblivion? Only the bitterest sting that life still has the power to inflict on him may shock him into facing the by now almost insuperable task of redeeming his power of response. In one of the novel's most poignant scenes Malraux unfolds for us Gisors' crisis which is brought on by Kyo's death. Will the deep, stinging grief awaken and disintoxicate the old man? Will it still succeed in wrenching him out of the clutches of his deceitful, poisonous god? For the last time Gisors faces a true challenge as he stands suspended in dread between the body of his dead son and his pipe. The darkness outside his window sharply contrasts with the light emanating from the room where Kyo is lying. In between, in a vague space of semidarkness, Gisors is fighting his greatest battle. The open door leading to Kyo's body beckons to show him the way he must choose, Kyo's way—the ascending path of dedication and sacrifice:

> For five minutes, Gisors had been looking at his pipe. Before him the lighted lamp ("which doesn't mean that I will use it"), the little box of opium, the clean needles. Outside, the night; in the room, the light of the small lamp and a great bright triangle at one end—the open doorway to the next room, where they had brought Kyo's body. . . . "All grief that helps no one is absurd," Gisors was thinking, hypnotized by his lamp, finding refuge in this fascination. "Peace is here. Peace." But he did not dare to advance his hand.[78]

As he looks up, he sees May, Kyo's wife. Her face and posture betray a grief so intense, she is so total, so living an embodiment of suffering—utterly incapable of feeling, thinking, or expressing anything outside or beyond this suffering—that

[78] *Ibid.*, pp. 329-30.

the sight of her startles and arouses him by its human immediacy:

> "And presently I shall have to wake up . . . ." How much longer would each morning bring this death back to him again? The pipe was there: peace. Advance his hand, prepare the pellet: after a few minutes, think of death itself with a limitless indulgence, as of some paralytic who might wish to harm him: it would no longer be able to reach him; it would lose its hold on him and would gently dissolve into the universal serenity. Liberation was there, within his reach.[79]

But he resists and with a resolute gesture throws the opium "into the night." He returns and, as for a wake which is simultaneously to be his own resurrection from death's kingdom, he sits down, "his shoulders drooping, waiting for the dawn . . . ." Deprived now of the last living link that tied him to life and bleeding from its loss, he is suddenly thrown back upon himself, and the awareness of it bears down upon him, intolerable and yet like a revelation, a mysterious expectation. "His love had to be crushed in order that he should discover that."[80] As he awaits the dawn, the night weighs heavily on him. Shaken to his entrails by his incredible loss, he accepts its weight and, for the duration of his sorrowful wake, fully reassumes the human condition:

> He felt the basic suffering trembling within him, not that which comes from creatures or from things, but that which gushes forth from man himself . . . . he could escape it, but only by ceasing to think of it; and he plunged into it deeper and deeper, as if this terrified contemplation were the only voice that death could hear, as if this suffering of

[79] *Ibid.,* p. 331.
[80] *Ibid.,* p. 332.

being a man which pervaded him, reaching down to the very depth of his heart, were the only prayer that the body of his dead son could hear.[81]

But the voice of human consciousness has no sooner rung out from within him to break death's evil spell, than it is silenced again. This time forever. The final and most imperious call, Kyo's death, has failed to produce in Gisors the longed-for metamorphosis of resurrection. At the end of the novel Malraux gives us a last glimpse of him, in Kobe. He is now not only a resigned victim, dwelling in the shadows of a saturnine infinite, but he actually blesses the very naught that encompasses him. Disdainful without reservations now of human existence, he says to May with the melancholy, angelic pride of an omniscient sage:

"Men should be able to learn that there is no reality, that there are worlds of contemplation—with or without opium —where all is vain. . . ." Liberated from everything, even from being a man, he caressed the stem of his pipe with gratitude, contemplating the bustle of all those unknown creatures who were marching toward death in the dazzling sunlight, each one nursing his deadly parasite in a secret recess of his being. "Every man is a madman," he went on thinking. . . . "Every man dreams of being god. . . ."[82]

Gisors floats in his illusory tower of contemplation from which, like Gide's Tityre, he looks out on the swamps in which creatures are swarming about. He is at the end of his journey; he has reached the bottom of gravity's descent. As he tells May, he now loves to listen to the strains of music, chanting of death. It is interesting to note here how much the young Malraux adhered to this Schopenhauerian notion of

81 *Ibid.*, pp. 332–33.
82 *Ibid.*, pp. 356, 357, 358.

music. Gisors' experience of music is closely related to the world of Wagnerian drama. The soul is dissolved in mythical enchantment which opens the gates not toward a higher, conscious ordering of experience but to the subterranean, uncreated pseudo infinity of magic and dreams.

The final image of Gisors falls well within the magic orbit of a "twilight of the gods." "Since Kyo died, I have discovered music," he confides to May, "music alone can speak of death."[83] From his window he watches the tiny shapes of men emerge from the port, streaming toward the city in preparation for a festival. He seems immune now against all things human, fixed within the double magic circle of opium and music. He seems to look out on the living figures from above, but Malraux unmistakably reveals to us this magically distilled "above" as the deepest circle of the "below": "Humanity was dense and heavy, heavy with flesh, with blood, with suffering, eternally clinging to itself like all that dies; but even blood, even flesh, even suffering, even death was being absorbed up there in the light like music in the silent night; the thought of Kama's music, and human grief seemed to rise and to lose itself in the very song of earth." Then the ecstasy dissolves and, like the other "conquerors," Gisors must finally face Saturn undisguised: "Upon the quivering release hidden within him like his heart, the grief which he had mastered slowly closed its inhuman arms."[84]

[83] *Ibid.*, p. 356.
[84] *Ibid.*, p. 358.

II

TWILIGHT

1

Voices

Malraux's "conquerors" have succumbed to the gravest temptation that befell both the *poètes maudits* and the German romantics; that of resolving or reducing the tension within the self by allowing an essential distinction to dissolve in both mind and imagination—the distinction between the self and the world. Contrary to the heroism of the poets, of Nerval, for example, who refused until the end of his life to let himself be dominated by his "voices," the "conquerors" have abandoned themselves to the subterranean "chant of death," and allowed it to transform the world into an echo which endlessly, monotonously, reverberates death's monologue. At the end of the diverse saturnine illuminations, Malraux shows us the silenced remains of madmen underneath the wrecks of the human city.

"Return to the city, return to the city!"[1] This cry of Kassner, the revolutionary hero of *The Days of Wrath*, fighting against madness in his solitary prison cell, might serve to mark a turning point in Malraux's work and in his conception of the hero.[2] Alongside and beyond the irremediable

---

[1] *Le Temps du Mépris* (Paris: Gallimard, 1935), p. 77.
[2] This is not to be understood chronologically. *Le Temps du Mépris*

predicament of his "conquerors," caught in a dark chaos which has engulfed the night of dream as well as the realm of day, he traces his heroes' quest for a more authentic human destiny. The basic condition for this quest imposes itself upon Kassner, upon Kyo, upon Manuel in *Man's Hope,* in the form of a sudden insight and acceptance: acceptance of the duality not only of the self but, subsequently, of the world, and finally of the self's relation to the world. From the closed circle in which a monologue has been echoing until all sounds have mingled and dissolved, Malraux leads his hero into an open dialogical situation.

Profoundly enough, it is in the closed cell and through music—that very medium which to Gisors confirmed doom —that Kassner becomes fully aware of the first and most essential task confronting him in his struggle to save himself out of the pit; namely, to recognize and uphold the clear distinction which exists between the realm of dream and the realm of human responsibility. This recognition comes to him with sudden clarity when, prey to an anxiety vision, he summons musical memories to his aid. In its effect upon him, the music reveals an unsuspected duality, a dual call: the one downward, toward the spirit's dissolution in a vague, undefined infinite; the other upward, toward a more articulate, more perfect order, in which man's vision of his destiny relates itself to and becomes one with its finite realization.

In Kassner's nightmare a vulture devours him, tearing out large chunks of his flesh with its sharp beak. The music he recalls to defend him holds off the bird of prey. But gradu-

---

was written in 1935, two years after *La Condition Humaine,* whose outstanding figures, as will be shown in this chapter, are the antiromantic heroes, Kyo and Katov.

ally he loses his hold on it and the music in turn now begins
to possess him. He has the feeling of sinking under the fascination of a funeral chant that rings in his ears, rings all around
him, becomes the anonymous voice of destiny that drowns
out time and memory.

> . . . and his youth, his pain, even his will, all vanished,
> revolving in a motionless course like that of the stars.
> Vulture and dungeon were plunged by the heavy cascade
> of the funeral chant into an infinite communion in which
> the music perpetuated all of the past by delivering it from
> time, by blending everything in its all-encompassing clar-
> ity, just as life and death melt and blend in the immobility
> of the starry sky.[3]

Everything, images, voices, shadows, "all his memory, dissolved in an endless rain . . . as if its inexhaustible downpour
had carried them away to the farthest depth of the past.
Death was perhaps like this music."[4] He is carried away on
the wings of this magic chant, floats, is dissolved until he
can no longer distinguish his body, his self, from the "endless
fatality of the stars." He gets up and, with pain in every
limb, slowly recovers awareness of his body, its shape, its
bones, its joints. And with this effort of recovering at all
cost his sense of reality which begins with the body, there
comes to him suddenly, like a gift, the knowledge that the
melodies are not only an invitation to deathly oblivion, but
that they have another, a life-giving, voice that invokes and
sustains man's virile responses to fate, his rebellion and communion with other men.

Trembling with concentration, Kassner listens for a fa-

[3] *Le Temps du Mépris,* p. 55.
[4] *Ibid.,* p. 55.

miliar appeal that may lead him back to the human City, protect the City from the apocalyptic invasion of thousands of riderless horses which, in a new delirium, he sees swooping down on it in a savage tumult until the earth opens underneath and swallows City and horses.

Only a few moments later he hears knocks on the wall coming from the adjoining cell. The at-first unintelligible, then clearly decipherable, voice of a fellow prisoner reaches him by means of those same walls that have spelled isolation, despair, and madness; it is as if in the depth of distress his struggle had prevailed upon a door suddenly to open, and allow him perhaps for the first time in full awareness to rejoin the human community.

If we move back from this episode to *Man's Fate,* we find there a crucial episode analogous in character, and by means of which Malraux explores further the implications of this discovery of life's dialogical nature. The episode which becomes the occasion of his hero Kyo's initiation into the consciously accepted role of leadership is in itself quite ordinary. Listening in Hemmelrich's phonograph shop to a recording he once made, Kyo is dismayed to discover that his own voice sounds totally unfamiliar to him. He is deeply shocked by this incident and his thoughts turn back to it persistently, seeking to clarify the puzzle. Slowly its meaning dawns on him: a human being is one thing to himself and something almost totally different to his fellow men. One hears his own voice from within—the private realm of dream; others hear it from without—the impersonal realm of action, and the two voices are strangely at odds. How to reconcile them? There seems to be no way in which they are related and yet both are part of himself. His father, to whom he confides his perplexity, does not grasp the essential problem, for to Gisors the inner world alone is real. He answers: "It's undoubtedly a question of means: we hear the voices of others with our ears." Kyo: "And our own?" Gisors: "With our throats: for you can hear your own voice with your ears stopped. Opium is also a world we do not hear with our ears. . . ."[5]

Kyo is not satisfied by this explanation. A contemplative like his father, keenly aware himself of an inner anguish and a calling within him to a divine, indefinable absolute, he is also a revolutionary leader who has committed himself unreservedly to action. From the moment when his own voice has rung out to him, unrecognizable and impersonal, the duality within him, the conflict between his being and his action, has become fully conscious and demands a solution. Up to that point it seems that he had simply accepted his role in the Shanghai uprising as the role naturally indicated for him by the political situation and his gifts of organization and leadership, and had accepted, just as naturally, his anguish, his "will to godhead," and his sense of separation from the people for whom he was risking his life. Easily for him too, the impersonal realm of action might have become a mere justification and disguise of private despair; like Ch'en for whom the scene of Chiang Kai-shek's assassination served as a stage for his private apocalypse of hatred, he too might have identified his despair with the revolutionary cause.

But Kyo, unlike the "conquerors," rejects this tempting confusion between the personal and the impersonal and refuses to use his actions as a mask for his inner demon. "I to myself, to my throat, what am I? A kind of absolute, the

[5] *Man's Fate,* trans. Haakon M. Chevalier (The Mod. Libr. edn.; New York: Random House, 1934), p. 48.

affirmation of an idiot: an intensity greater than that of all the rest. To others I am what I have done."[6] Once this distinction is firmly established in his mind, the question is: is there no link between the two, no analogy between the inner self and those "others," that may make a dialogue between them possible? If his aloneness, his sense of estrangement from others, were absolute, then Kyo like Garine or Perken, must needs die of hatred and despair. But there is one being, his wife, to whom he is neither the sum of what he does, as to the world, nor that incomprehensible monster that he is to himself. To May he is he, Kyo whom she loves; that is, accepts unquestioningly, in an intimate communion.

Since his mother had died, May was the only being for whom he was not Kyo Gisors, but an intimate partner. "A partnership consented, conquered, chosen," he thought, extraordinarily in harmony with the night, as if his thoughts were no longer made for the light. "Men are not my kind, there are those who look at me and judge me; my kind are those who love me and do not look at me, who love me in spite of everything, degradation, meanness, treason—*me* and not what I have done or shall do—who would love me as long as I would love myself—even to suicide . . . with her alone I have this love in common, injured or not, as others have children who are ill and in danger of dying. . . ." It was not happiness, certainly. It was something primitive which was at one with the darkness and caused a warmth to rise in him, resolving itself into a motionless embrace, as of cheek against cheek, the only thing in him that was as strong as death.[7]

"Strong as death," yet frail as all things human, Kyo's love for May—anchor on which his entire being is grounded—is

6 *Ibid.,* p. 59.
7 *Ibid.,* pp. 59–60.

menaced at every moment, by every whim of circumstance. She has just caused him pangs of jealousy and distress through a trivial incident and immediately the bond of love that links him to her chafes like a prisoner's chain. But he does not allow himself to be blinded by this: "No, even at this moment he was sure that if she were to die he would no longer serve his cause with hope but with despair, as though he himself were dead."[8]

Having recognized the almost silent but powerful call to communion in his personal destiny and having accepted its challenge and promise, Kyo is free to direct his attention to the outside, to the world of "strangers." His ensuing dialogue with it does not differ essentially from that which he carries on with May. His fate is bound up with the fate of the world of men around him because he shares with them the prisoner's estate. This bond may easily give rise to hatred; but it may also create fraternal compassion. It all depends upon whether he further imprisons himself in his "monstre de rêve" and consequently has to negate the City or whether, having accepted his own duality, he can accept the duality inherent in others, the "strangers," and choose to confront them, not as hostile masters or victims, but as cosufferers and cofighters. Kyo makes his choice consciously, deliberately, and henceforth his words and actions speak with a clear and powerful resonance that sets them apart from the ambiguous activity of the "conquerors":

Ch'en . . . had found himself without money, provided only with worthless diplomas, with his twenty-four years and China before him. . . . Everything had pushed him into political activity: the hope of a different world, the

[8] *Ibid.*, p. 52.

possibility of eating, though wretchedly . . . , the grati-
fication of his hatreds, his mind, his character. This activity gave a meaning to his solitude. But with Kyo everything was simpler. The heroic sense had given him a kind
of discipline, not a kind of justification of life. He was
not restless. His life had a meaning, and he knew what it
was: to give to each of these men whom famine, at this
very moment, was killing off like a slow plague, the sense
of his own dignity. . . . " There is no possible dignity,
no real life for a man who works twelve hours a day without knowing why he works." That work would have to
take on a meaning, become a faith. Individual problems
existed for Kyo only in his private life.[9]

So we find him, and also Katov, lending his voice to the
silent mass of men, victims of every kind of physical and
spiritual distress, joining in their chorus of lamentation,
calling them to rebellion.

The voices of death are many in *Man's Fate*, but they are
no longer unbroken echoes of an all-pervading monologue.
In the great moments of the novel, a human voice is now
heard in heroic answer, either quietly countering Saturn's
threat or joining freely out of fraternal compassion in the
dirge of the dying.

At one moment we hear the armored train of the Blues
going into action to rout the revolutionary army which is
entering Shanghai. Katov stands near the train. An armored
train, as he knows from previous battles, is a thing of such
hellish terror that no human courage is strong enough to
resist it. But this time he will resist it. By a supreme act of
will he masters his nerves and succeeds in standing up to the
deathly roar.

[9] *Ibid.*, p. 70.

Again, in one of the last scenes of the novel and certainly
its climax, we find Kyo and Katov lying in a large hall,
waiting among hundreds of others to be killed by Chiang
Kai-shek's police. Most of the men will be shot; these two
and a few others are to be burned alive in the boiler of a
locomotive waiting nearby at the station. Every time a man
is thrown into the boiler the locomotive whistles. In between
are heard the groans and murmurs of the condemned most
of whom are wounded. In this last hour of agony, Kyo
listens to these men around him whose rebels' fate he has
consented to share. His destiny has become one with theirs
and it is now being consummated in the sacrifice of his life.
He accepts this death. It will not be a defeat but a consecration, his own humble consecration of what he believes to be
the fundamental meaning of human destiny: love. For love
alone can withstand and transcend, however fleetingly, both
that fearful uproar and the equally fearful silence of imprisonment.

> This place of agony was no doubt the most weighed with
> virile love. He could wail with this crowd of prostrate
> men, join this sacrificed suffering even in its murmur of
> complaint. . . . And an inaudible chorus of lamentation
> prolonged this whispering of pain into the depth of the
> night. . . . It is easy to die when one does not die alone.[10]

After Kyo is dead, having swallowed the cyanide which
all the leaders keep concealed in the buckle of their belts,
Katov remains alone between his dead friend on one side and
two young Chinese, also condemned to burning, on the other.
Once more he is summoned to answer, this time simultaneously, the voice of destruction (in the sound of the whistle)

[10] *Ibid.*, p. 322.

and the outcry of human anguish. The two young men are weeping with fear, without a sob. With only a few more moments to live, forsaken himself and in the grip of terror, he wrenches himself free once again, and, in a gesture that transforms his entire destiny into a triumph of human compassion, hands over his cyanide to the two young men: "In spite of the hum, in spite of all those men who had fought as he had, Katov was alone, alone between the body of his dead friend and his two terror-stricken companions, alone between this wall and that whistle far off in the night. But a man could be stronger than this solitude and even, perhaps, than that atrocious whistle. . . ."[11] When the two young men have died the quick death induced by the powerful poison, the guards come to lead him out next. "All the heads . . . followed the rhythm of his walk, with love, with dread, with resignation."[12] The sound of his footsteps is surrounded by a deep, breathless silence, the voice of wordless communion.

This wordless communion sustains men not only in the face of terror; it has the life-giving power of transforming humiliation and self-hatred into hope and trust. We find an example of this in a simple earlier episode. Katov arrives at Hemmelrich's shop just after the latter has refused out of fear to harbor Ch'en and his fellow-terrorists with their bombs. Hemmelrich is mortified with shame and self-contempt and ready to murder Katov. With the wailing of Hemmelrich's sick child in the background, Katov silently listens to the other man, listens not so much to his violent words but to the profound distress they conceal. With a few

[11] *Ibid.*, pp. 325–26.
[12] *Ibid.*, p. 329.

quiet remarks, without trying to console or justify him, he reaches through the tenacious wall of hatred that the shop-keeper has put up, shares the nameless misery behind it and gives it a voice, thus ennobling it and restoring it to the common fund of human sorrow.

To give a voice to the silent grief of men, to articulate and compose their inarticulate hopes and ecstasies even at the risk of losing his own voice, his personal dreams and long-ings—this same task confronts the hero of Malraux's epic novel about the Spanish Civil War, *Man's Hope*.

Elsewhere, Malraux has described the artist's long strug-gle, the intense dialogue that he carries on for years with his destiny—his tradition, his temperament, his vocation—before he finally speaks with his own voice and through it, in a language that transcends the personal vocabulary, speaks not only for himself but for his people and his time.

Malraux's revolutionary heroes, particularly Manuel in *Man's Hope*, can be seen to follow the same dialectical path. They are in more than one way prefigurations of the con-cept of the artist as Malraux later developed it in *The Voices of Silence*. But we shall see that, whereas the artist finds his voice along the path of "creative rebellion," the hero loses his in a battle that is foredoomed by its very nature.

Like Kyo, the young Manuel has accepted the necessity of learning to draw a clear line of distinction between his own "romantic fancies" and the "verifiable realities" of the situation at hand. He too goes through an experience of initiation: an execution, ordered and witnessed by him, of two civil guards. He comes out of it profoundly shocked and with a new and weighty awareness of the "birth of responsibility" that has taken place within him. The responsibility, so suddenly and clearly facing this young, essentially aloof and complex intellectual,[13] is that of attuning himself to the obscure if powerful rumblings of the people's suffering and rebellion, and of becoming their spokesman and defender. This is a heroic task. It involves creating order or what Malraux calls a "style" out of that "apocalypse" of hope which would otherwise hopelessly succumb to its own irrational, romantic passion, its inner contradictions and, above all, to the saturnine voice of cruelty and mechanized destruction of the Fascist conquerors.

Even more manifold than in *Man's Fate,* the sounds of death and suffering throughout *Man's Hope* evoke dread and compassion. Most symbolic perhaps of the blind, helpless confusion of the people under the mechanized attacks of the enemy is the bleating of the sheep around the Prado, after the all-out bombing of Madrid: "up to the limit of the light a flock of sheep was surging around. There seemed no end to it; they could hear bleat after bleat far into the distance. And not a trace of a shepherd."[14]

It takes Manuel all his newly acquired sense of dedication not to close his ears when he hears for the first time the agonizing screams of the wounded in the San Carlos Hospital, where he visits one of his men.

From the bed in the center of the room came endless moans of pain, pain so intense as to transcend all human speech, the suffering that wrings from the sufferer those

[13] Since several Malraux critics have already amply demonstrated this, it does not seem necessary to point out once more how much the major characters resemble each other and Malraux himself.

[14] *Man's Hope,* trans. Stuart Gilbert and Alastair Macdonald (New York: Random House, 1938), p. 393.

cries of wordless agony which are common to both man
and beast; that succession of hoarse screams, rising and
falling with the breath, which gives the impression that
they can only end when the breath itself gives out. And
when at last they did stop, they were followed by a grind-
ing of the teeth . . . appalling to listen to.[15]

He is aghast. It seems to him that the cries of the wounded
flier, "would be part of this room for eternity,"[16] "that pain
had set up its kingdom here for all eternity, beyond time and
the world."[17]

Not only in this hospital but over all of Spain bloodied by
victims and fire, the voice of death is heard. Malraux re-
creates for us a veritable holocaust through the sounds alone:
screaming sirens, dirges, "barbarous litanies," lamentations
sung by the people in the streets of cities and villages, the
whimpering and screaming of the wounded, howling stray
dogs, exploding bombs, roaring guns, crashing window-
panes and buildings, shrilly ringing clocks; the cadence of
the rain, the silences of dreadful anticipations and ghostly
aftermaths, the frightened chorus of hundreds of cocks
crowing at dawn.

To all these, the people respond with tunes of blind,
delirious hope and courage, none of which is more revealing
than the repeatedly-heard playing of the "International" by
the blind beggars of Madrid, on the eve of one of the most
devastating Fascist attacks. When the Republicans score their
first successes, the triumphant crowd of Madrid shouts
Salud "in a never-ending chorus of fraternity." "The Republican hymn blaring from all radios, songs of all kinds,

15 *Ibid.*, p. 90.
16 *Ibid.*, p. 91.
17 *Ibid.*, p. 89.

cries of 'Salud' . . . mingled like the notes of a piano—
sounds of hope and exultation filled the night."[18] Again,
when the International Brigade seeks to stem the advance of
the Moors, a triumphant dialogue is heard rising above all
barriers of communication: "a blackbird's song rose through
the air in seeming interrogation—and drew an answer."[19]
The "blackbirds" are Siry and Kogan, two men of the
Brigade, one a Frenchman, the other a Bulgarian who speaks
no French. So they question and answer each other, the answer meaning "they shall not pass." Their forces finally
succeed in driving the Moors back across the Manganares
river: "A blackbird broke into ecstatic song. Somewhere in
the mist, his life blood gushing out on to the fallen leaves
. . . Kogan answered for the wounded, for the dead."[20]

Throughout the epic narration of the war, the romantic
element, the people's boundless hope, bursts into expression
time and again, rising above the growing thunder of planes
and machine guns. Moreno, one of the young anarchists—
the "romantics" of the revolution—relates a front-line battle
he has been in, a battle where every man on his side was
doomed in advance:

> Yes, that's how it is, one pushes ahead into the barrage;
> nothing, not even one's own life, makes the least differ-
> ence. Hundreds of shells are falling, hundreds of men
> going forward. You're just another case of suicide, yet at
> that moment you're sharing in something that's best in
> all of them. You're sharing in something that's rather like
> the ecstasy of the crowd at Carnival. I wonder if you see
> what I mean. . . . I've a pal who calls that the moment

18 *Ibid.*, p. 112.
19 *Ibid.*, p. 330.
20 *Ibid.*, p. 338.

when the dead start singing. Yes, for a month now, I've
known that dead men can sing.[21]

This exaltation of the human element inherent in the
common fight, this joy in a "personal apocalypse" of fraternity marks the "adolescence of revolution." This element,
above all, the leader must subdue and transform for, given
the lead, it never fails to bring about defeat. "The apocalyptic mood clamours for everything right away," says Garcia,
whose great organizing intelligence shapes and disciplines
the minds of the men around him throughout the novel.
"That apocalyptic fervour is ingrained in every one of us;
and there's the danger. For that fervour spells certain defeat,
after a relatively short period, and for a very simple reason:
it's in the very nature of an apocalypse to have no future . . .
Even when it professes to have one. . . . Our humble task
is to *organize* the apocalypse."[22]

It is a humble, but above all a tragic, task. Taught by the
experience of the war itself and by his monitors, Garcia,
Ximenes, and Guernico, officers older than himself and to
whom he stands in an almost filial relation, Manuel gradually
assumes the tragic stature of a leader who knows about the
duality; more than that, who knows about the insoluble
paradox of all purely temporal or historical endeavor—the
ideal and the means employed toward realizing this ideal
contradict each other hopelessly, one defeating the other.
The choice which he must make then is this: adhere to the
ideals for which the Republicans are fighting, justice, brother-
hood, the preservation of the "quality of man," and lose the
battle against the conquerors; or sacrifice this ideal in order

21 *Ibid.*, p. 370.
22 *Ibid.*, p. 118.

to win, and attune himself fully to the demands of the situation from moment to moment.

In terms of his personal destiny, this means that he must choose between an inner voice that calls him to self-realization and self-transcendence by upholding and purifying the people's cause, and the more efficient but dehumanized voice of expediency. As Manuel grows in responsibility, we hear him gradually exchange his true voice for the voice of command. "I don't give a damn what a man is," he says to Alba, "it's what he does that counts with me."[23] Gradually we see and hear him grow paler as a figure. Persistently forced to reduce himself, by an effort of pure will, to an impersonal agent of the Revolution, he loses his passion and his vibrancy, and becomes one-dimensional.[24] We hear Manuel issue commands to his troops: "He had picked up the language of command as one picks up a foreign language, by repetition."[25] Manuel is in a far more tragic position than Kyo, for whom this same conflict has been resolved in the sacrifice of his own life. He, being called upon to live and command, which means to impose judgment on others, has to suffer and accept the gap that grows within him between his vision and being—the "human quality" so ardently defended by the anarchists—and the impersonal efficiency demanded of him as a communist. This painful split grows

23 *Ibid.*, p. 166.
24 It might be in order here to point to the striking difference in character between the episodes cited in "Saturnalia" and those in this chapter. The latter must strike the reader as dramatically far less impressive. This difference corresponds to the intrinsic difference of quality that separates Malraux's initial movement of passion from this transitional twilight phase, which is essentially given over to an elucidation of the will, and subsequently is richer in insights and deliberations than in images and true dramatic power.
25 *Man's Hope*, p. 244.

until, suddenly, one day (he later refers to it as the most important day of his life) he discovers that he has literally lost his voice, that is, his inner self.

The crucial episode is this: two men of his brigade who have attempted to run away under fire have been condemned to be shot.

> Manuel wondered what he could say to them. The argument for their defense was something inexpressible in words; it was in that streaming face, that open mouth which had made Manuel aware that there was the everlasting face of the man who pays. Never had he realized so keenly the necessity of choosing between victory and compassion.[26]

He faces them in helpless silence. That afternoon, when he has to address his men, he is hoarse. "He had been shouting all day; but that alone could not account for his voicelessness."[27] Someone comes to inform him that the execution will take place in the evening. "By now, Manuel had lost his voice altogether."[28] He has to scribble his next statement on a pad for someone else to read it to the men. It is the announcement of a victory.

The next morning, when his soldiers march past him in formation, their eyes pay tribute to him with an expression of "tragic fraternity," pay tribute to the one who has died to himself to take charge of their common fight. "Never had Manuel felt so much alone."[29] He walks over to Ximenes to tell him what has happened and confide to him his sense of loss and estrangement. "Every day I am getting a little less

26 *Ibid.*, p. 390.
27 *Ibid.*, p. 404.
28 *Ibid.*
29 *Ibid.*, p. 406.

human."[30] He bitterly states to his friend the inevitable result of revolutionary and wartime dialectic. The thing he is
pledged to defend becomes more and more of an abstraction,
defeating in turn the very men it claims to defend: "To be
linked more closely to the Party is worthless, if one's to be
estranged from the very men for whom the Party's working.
Whatever the Party is aiming at, that aim exists only as the
aim of each and every one of us. One of these condemned
men said to me: 'Ah, so you've no voice now, so far as we're
concerned!'"[31] Ximenes points out to him that this conflict
is analogous to the one every man is up against within himself, that there is always a choice to be made. "The real
struggle begins when you have to contend against a part of
your own self. Up to that point it's all plain sailing. But it's
only from such inner conflicts that a real man emerges. Yes,
we've always got to fear the world within ourselves; there's
no escaping it."[32]

This reply, true in part, advocates in fact an abdication.
It signifies the choice of expediency and organization against
the very heart and core of the Loyalist cause—the fight to
defend for the Spanish people the human element in life,
the "quality of man" attacked by the conquerors. Manuel
knows all too well that the preservation of the human quality
can alone give a meaning to the bloodshed of the civil war.
The same doubt besets him that makes the old art historian
Alvear wonder aloud while the machine guns are blasting
outside in the streets: "What's to prove that the benefits the
'economic liberation' they talk about may bring, will be

[30] *Ibid.*, p. 408.
[31] *Ibid.*, p. 409.
[32] *Ibid.*

greater than the losses entailed by the new order—threatened
as it's sure to be on every side, and scared into acts of violence, repression, perhaps treachery."[33]

Manuel's distress is deepened when another of his fellow
officers, Heinrich, after listening to him, calmly reflects:

> "From the day you take a commission in the army of the
> proletariat, your soul is no longer your own . . . you must
> lose your soul. You've already lost your long hair—and
> the sound of your voice has changed. . . . All victories in-
> volve losses . . . and not only on the battle field." He
> gripped Manuel's arm, and added in a voice which might
> have been bitter or merely practical and firm—Manuel
> could not guess which: "And now, you must never again
> waste pity on a lost man."[34]

In Manuel's destiny, the first in Malraux's work not to
end in death, a heavy tribute is paid by the hero to the
saturnine forces which seek to conquer him and his cause
from without and within. The toll is paid consciously and
proudly, but it leaves him standing on the very edge of the
precipice of spiritual death. He finds himself cut off both
from his past (his memories, his dreams), and from a future
which he can no longer conceive. More and more stripped
of all sense of anticipation as the rigid impersonality of his
role bears down on him, he is forced to stake his life on the
slender moments of an immediate present.

In a mood of farewell, farewell to what was once himself,
that small voice of hope and the dream of human fulfillment,
Manuel listens to Beethoven's "Les Adieux." Its flow and
completeness remove him for a few instants from the imperious realm of action which he has chosen, and allow him

[33] *Ibid.*, p. 322.
[34] *Ibid.*, p. 411.

to meditate on its perilous tentativeness: "Like the sleep-walker who wakes up suddenly on the edge of a roof, he felt the dying cadence of the music bringing home to him the terrible precariousness of his mental foothold; any false step might land him in—a shambles!"[35] He seems to feel no despair at this indefinite suspension of his being; he accepts the necessity of living this way, from act to act and from moment to moment, determined to draw from the very hopelessness of man's struggle the full measure of courage and rebellion.

> For the first time Manuel was hearing the voice of that which is more awe-inspiring even than the blood of men, more enigmatic even than their presence on the earth— the infinite possibilities of their destiny. And he felt that this new consciousness within him was linked up with the sounds of running water in the street and the footfalls of the prisoners, profound and permanent as the beating of his heart.[36]

No despair certainly, but an infinite resignation speaks out of these lines. Manuel's voice has lost its personal resonance and has assumed the same quality of fatalism that colors all history and its movements. This voice can at best maintain itself against Saturn's fascination; it is bound to remain essentially helpless against his power.

[35] *Ibid.*, pp. 509–10.
[36] *Ibid.*, p. 511.

2

Darkness and Light

Darkness, it seemed, would steal a march on Marcelino's homing plane—and night landings are not recommended for wounded pilots. The ground staff seemed lost in contemplation of the nightfall; but what they were watching in hushed suspense, under the tranquil menace of the dusk, was the unseen race between the airmen and the advancing night.[37]

The drama of man's "panic conquest . . . not of a world of dreams but of the star-strewn darkness which broods upon the august presence of the Mothers or the slumber of the gods"[38] is no longer confined in *Man's Hope* to the destiny of one hero. Manuel clarifies the terms of man's "dialogue with fate," but neither he nor any one of the other leaders can by himself sustain man's voice in it. Beyond the part played by the hero in the battle against Saturn, and sustaining his part, the Promethean flight of the people's planes is seen rising into that "starlit night," to confront and resist there, in its bosom, the two faces of death: the magic circle of infinite silence, and the fire-spitting bombs (the con-

37 *Man's Hope,* p. 158.
38 "Museum without Walls," *The Voices of Silence,* trans. Stuart Gilbert (Garden City: Doubleday, 1953), p. 63.

queror's bombs) laying waste the human city in apocalyptic visitations of dread. We witness a dialogue between a nocturnal saturnine heaven and the world of men. In its course the evil spirits are hounded down to earth and encountered there in a holocaust of fire which spells both destruction and purification, certain death but also the promise of resurrection.

As in the "conqueror" novels, darkness predominates in *Man's Hope* until the very end, steeping the scene in a "grave, unfathomable gloom."[39] But now we find an indeterminate quality about it, a duality and a suspension. The night is seen advancing steadily over Spain as do the conquerors' armies, yet within this night there is the "dark, underground communion" of the people rejoicing, amidst terror and devastation, in a Promethean "carnival of liberty."[40] Destruction is countered by a reckless hope of victory and liberation that will not be deterred by any cost or punishment.

Time and again, in what Scali, the art historian-turned-bomber, designates as a "fight to the death with death,"[41] Prometheus, having ravished fire from the jealous gods, is himself destroyed by the fire of the deadly heaven, or spent by his own consuming passion. Several of the most breathtaking of these duels between Prometheus and Saturn are fought in the air, realm of the gods. We have the bombing of Toledo's Alcazar, the stronghold of the fascists, by Marcelino and his companions. As the plane climbs, it seems to take flight from the earth and to be drawn into the heavenly

39 *Man's Hope*, p. 80.
40 *Ibid.*, p. 47.
41 *Ibid.*, p. 322.

orbit which is impervious to human existence. "An un-
heeded atom in the vast cosmic movement, the aeroplane
gyrated like a tiny planet."[42] Through a rift in the clouds
the Alcazar becomes visible and instantly the plane is transformed back into a bird of prey: "like a circling hawk the
plane swung round and round, prospecting for a larger
opening, the gaze of all on board set vigilantly earthwards."[43]
It swoops down and drops the first bomb. Before Marcelino
can give the signal for the releasing of the second bomb,
white sheets are seen; the Alcazar is surrendering.

But hours later as night is falling, the men at the airport
are still anxiously waiting for the plane to return. When it
is finally heard approaching in almost total darkness, it is
seen standing out against the sky as if against a glare of foot-
lights. A wing is on fire. "All eyes were gazing only at the
shapeless mass of the fuselage on which the fierce blue flame
of a steel-welder's blowpipe seemed battering like some bird
of prey. The landing was interminably protracted; planes
freighted with the dead are slow to take the earth."[44] Once a
punishing bird of prey, the plane has been turned into prey
after its bold venture, and atones for its moment's glory in a
return foredoomed by fire: "Just as the machine touched
earth, fuselage and flames interlocked in the last furious
round of a struggle to the death. The body of the plane
crashed down on to the flame which writhed and flattened
out, then leapt up again with a hissing roar. Then the machine turned turtle."[45] Three men dead, three wounded, the
last one blind. "Their comrades huddled round them in a

42 *Ibid.*, p. 145.
43 *Ibid.*
44 *Ibid.*, p. 160.
45 *Ibid.*, p. 161.

chequerwork of shadows; under the spectral glare the watch-
ers moved like unquiet corpses watching the quiet dead."[46]

Nostalgia grips the men who gaze into the faces of their
dead comrades. Life recedes and becomes unreal as, with
the smoothing away of wrinkles and crow's feet, the "true
face" of death begins to show "across the mask of life."[47] This
nostalgia for the silent aloofness of death also grips Garcia
who watches the Alcazar where Fascists and Loyalists are
interlocked in a fierce battle of dynamite and machine guns,
under a "dazzling effulgence that merged living and dead
together in a holocaust of light."[48] "The vibrant frenzy of
the air throbbed in Garcia's body; the intense glare and heat
almost made him vomit."[49] His eyes fall on the nearby grave-
yard with its pale stones and monuments, and he longs with
all his being for that peace and "intimation of eternity" that
makes human struggles seem ridiculous and futile.

Death's power of seduction draws men not only to the
pale underworld; it is experienced even more irresistibly in
the "godlike freedom" of the plane floating through space.
Leclerc, one of the mercenary fliers of the Pelican Squadron, takes off on a night flight in an old defective machine
to bomb the Talavera gas works. His nerves geared to his
dangerous task, in his precariously functioning plane, he is
yet seized by the exultant feeling of omnipotence emanating
from the nocturnal sky which releases him as if by magic
from his human condition and concerns: "It was a freedom
greater than sleep and war, greater than pain and passion."[50]

46 *Ibid.*
47 *Ibid.*
48 *Ibid.*, p. 129.
49 *Ibid.*, p. 127.
50 *Ibid.*, p. 216.

With the approach of the target, the earth summons him and his crew and they blow up the gas works in a feat of precision bombing. The Promethean task accomplished, the plane takes to the heights again and is reabsorbed by timeless space.

After every effort to harness the fire in man's defence, every encounter between "human plenitude and the power of death,"[51] we see the night descend slowly on the world of men, "making their never-ending struggles seem infinitely vain, lost in the spate of darkness, the massive indifference of the earth,"[52] and we see the Promethean figures take refuge and consolation in this very vanity. The call of life, once heeded, seems to liberate the longing for death in an alternation that is like the alternation of night and day, of the eternal cosmic cycle and the realm of human time, until night overcomes the day. This is particularly true in the battles waged by the "romantic" anarchists for whom life is a proposition of "all or nothing." Their passionate attacks in the blazing light of day are followed by an even more passionate surrender to the repose of darkness, as if the day were but a prelude or life but a mask of death. We see Hernandez, whose nobility and compassion have won him the bewildered admiration of his own men and his Fascist enemies, remain behind in Toledo with a handful of his men, having refused to save himself and be separated from them. As the Moorish cavalry pours into Toledo, he takes hold of a machine gun and covers the last street through which his men may still flee to safety. "The last Republicans vanished up the

51 "La Création Artistique," *Les Voix du Silence* (Paris: Galerie de la Pléiade, NRF, 1951), p. 462.
52 *Man's Hope,* p. 172.

street in a confused mass, treading on each other's heels. His mind void of thoughts, Hernandez pressed his shoulders to the butt of his gun; he was utterly happy, happy without reserve."[53]

This moment of supreme self-sacrifice for the sake of love, this epiphany of joy, is rendered by Malraux as an almost infallible prelude to death's advent, and rightly so, for to the romantic, especially the intellectual romantic like Hernandez, love by no means signifies love of life and the human world; rather it is an absolute affirmation of a meaning or value that is bound to turn against life by making it seem impossible. "No one was left in the bull ring. At last he, too, jumped down. A glancing blow, like a whiplash, seared his forehead; he felt his eyes growing blurred with blood. Another blow crashed down on his back. . . ."[54] The ensuing scenes of Hernandez' imprisonment and execution are close in character to Kyo's last scenes; only, unlike Kyo, Hernandez is spent, and he welcomes death as a deliverance. He refuses to take a last chance to break loose and save himself. "He was too tired, and tired of life as well. It would mean an effort, another effort."[55] With relief his eyes rest on the fresh-turned earth while he waits his turn to face the firing squadron: "Earth inert, reposeful . . . only living men are torn by anguish and disgust."[56]

The Negus, famous anarchist, most clearly expresses this romantic urge to appropriate the fire here and now, heedless of the price to be paid, and the impatience that prevents the rebel from being able to accept human destiny as a gradual

[53] *Ibid.*, p. 248.
[54] *Ibid.*
[55] *Ibid.*, p. 255.
[56] *Ibid.*, p. 258.

unraveling, a slow metamorphosis of dark chaos into light:
"We've no use for 'dialectics' . . . what we are out for is to
live the way men ought to live, right now and here; or else
to damn well die. If we fail, there's an end of it. No return
ticket for me!"[57] The Negus's disgust is certainly felt rather
than thought, yet his heart is swayed by the same rationalist
demon that made Ivan Karamazov reject "God's world," and
want to turn in his ticket because of a single tear shed by an
innocent child. This apocalypse of love is as quickly defeated
as the "conqueror's" apocalypse of hatred. It is but a small
spark of a purely natural fire against the demonic conflagration kindled by the gods' wrath, an ephemeral moment engulfed all too soon by the eternal cycle of time. What indeed
is the plenitude, even of an almost miraculously luminous
moment, against the sinister "time-of-history" which turns
all dreams to derision?

All the glory and the hopelessness of this love of the heart
against the hostile divinity is rendered marvelously in a
scene in which the little man Mercery helps fight the fires
started all over Madrid by the conquerors' incendiary bombs:

> Mercery felt quite Napoleonic. He tugged his moustache
> cheerfully. . . . "Come on, lads. Up the ladders again! The
> fire is picking up. Come on, lads! For the People, and for
> Liberty!" . . . He aimed the nozzle of the hose. The seeth-
> ing mass of flames on which he played it was the fiercest of
> all. It was an enemy with more life in it than any man,
> more life than anything else in the world. Facing this
> enemy of a myriad writhing tentacles, like a fantastic octo-
> pus, Mercery felt he was terribly slow, as though made of
> lead. But for all its tentacles, he would best the monster.
> Behind him avalanches of smoke were pouring, black and

[57] *Ibid.*, pp. 200–201.

garnet-red. Through all the noises of the conflagration he could hear people coughing in the street, scores and scores of them. He seemed floundering in a dry, dazzling sea of incandescence. The patch of fire died down. The last smoke-wisp lifted, and Mercery could see Madrid below in a lightless pit. All lights had been extinguished and the town was outlined only by the distant fires, flapping like bull-fighters, their scarlet capes across the darkness. He had given up all, even Madame Mercery, to help to make a better world. He pictured himself stopping with a gesture those little children's hearses, white and quaintly decorated like wedding-cakes. For him, each explosion he heard, each fire he saw, meant those poor, heartbreaking little hearses.[58]

This "love of the heart" aspect of romanticism which complements the "conqueror" tradition of metaphysical rebellion has its own fatal flaw. Mercery embodies the rational agnosticism and optimism which, since Rousseau, has been seeking to turn love into a means of attaining justice, "forgetting that the love preached on the Mount was not of the heart but of the spirit, not sentimental but metaphysical, and that it had spread all over Europe not because it claimed to reconcile men, but because it claimed to wrench them from an earth gorged with death."[59] In more than one scene, Malraux depicts in *Man's Hope* the profound ineffectiveness which the nineteenth-century social utopia was to show in the face of the metaphysical problem of death and "its peremptory expression, cruelty."[60] The vision he gives us of a Madrid "veiled in the shroud of its conflagration,"[61] under

[58] *Ibid.*, pp. 400–401.
[59] *Saturne: Essai sur Goya* (1st edn.; Paris: Galerie de la Pléiade, NRF, 1950), p. 111.
[60] *Ibid.*
[61] *Man's Hope*, p. 409.

clouds that seem to have welled up from an "unseen furnace," or of a Toledo where the houses are "burning their hearts out tranquilly,"[62] corresponds to another striking image in *The Voices of Silence,* which depicts a Europe devastated precisely by the mania to reduce man to his social or historical, sentimental or rational, dimension in the traditions of Rousseau and Hegel:

> This Europe of phantom cities is not herself more devastated than is the concept of Man that once was hers. Squatting like Parcae in their museums going up in flames, prescient fetishes watched the gutted cities of a West now grown akin to the primitive world that gave them birth, mingling their last thin wisps of smoke with the dense clouds rising from the death ovens.[63]

The anarchist's passion for establishing a kingdom of heaven on earth, his quixotic "illusion of a miracle" is but a fool's paradise, like the "conqueror's" illusion of magic; it is a venture into fate's whirling orbit without the possibility of a return. "Look at 'em!" Moreno calls out to Hernandez in disgust as he watches a crowd of battle-happy *milicianos:*

> "A pack of lunatics! . . . Look at them, damn it! All those fellows simpering at each other: 'I am a thinker, I'm making history.' Kisses. Slapping each other on the back. But put 'em in a cell . . . and then what? Pennies tossed in the air. When I escaped I was crazy about getting back; I reported at once for duty. Now I know better. No one on earth can escape what's coming to him, *his truth.* And it isn't death, no, it isn't even suffering. . . . It's the spin of a coin, of a penny."[64]

62 *Ibid.,* p. 197.
63 "Aftermath of the Absolute," p. 541.
64 *Man's Hope,* p. 227.

The despair from which Moreno suffers at that moment is the inevitable reaction that prevents the romantic from going beyond that "spin of a coin." His despair stems from his inability to sustain the miracle of hope. Gradually Malraux leads his heroes to learn to sustain it, as, in the growing warmth of a true communion, they pool their own light-giving and sustaining power of insight and organization with the people's blind, strong faith. From the image of the closed circle or circles, we come to the repeatedly recurring image of the tunnel—symbol of man's venture through darkness toward a new dawn. In the traversing of the dread tunnel, the holocaust of destruction becomes a purifying School of Fire. Men's past, their grief, their crushed hopes are revivified and reshaped there in a fundamental confrontation "in which fate ends and man comes into his own,"[65] in which he learns to face, without being blinded by them, the cosmos and the nocturnal powers.

In the little village of San Isidro, Manuel stands inside the old church now wrecked by flames. "What savage grandeur was in those convulsed statues that somehow had outlived the holocaust! It was as if the flames had set them dancing in the church and their agony had given birth to a new school of art, the school of fire."[66] Drawn together by the fire, the intellectuals and the humble people pool their hopes for the birth of a new style, as Lopez the artist puts it—a style that would express "the spirit of man engaged in mortal conflict,"[67] and a new epiphany of the Lord

---

[65] "Museum without Walls," *The Voices of Silence*, p. 75.
[66] *Man's Hope*, p. 174.
[67] *Ibid.*, p. 44.

of love which the peasant Gustavo invokes at the end of his improvisation:

> and they understood in their hearts that Our Lord was living there, among the poor and oppressed ones of the earth . . . and when the slaughtering had gone too far and the last company of the poor had set out on the march . . . a new Star rose above them.[68]

In several crucial episodes we witness battles against the destroying fire in the sinister darkness of tunnels and corridors—perfect images of hell. Through Malraux's compelling sense of the sacred, each of these scenes assumes a metaphysical significance; persistently and deliberately he relates "le détail à la profondeur," in the fashion of his great Spanish ancestor.

The first of these tunnel scenes is the most ghastly: a face-to-face encounter between some Republican *milicianos* and their leaders, and a group of Fascists advancing toward them, preceded by a flame thrower. It is like a venture into the livid fire of hell from which return seems impossible; but, having wrenched the flame thrower out of the enemy's hands, and guided by a glimmer of light at the far end of the tunnel, those who have survived the holocaust of flames succeed in crossing the long stretch of darkness and return to the world of daylight.

> Before them loomed a large tunnel-like corridor in which the smoke glowed red. The din of the battle going on outside was hardly audible here and the fumes of burning gasoline had effectively dispelled the stench of carrion. The fascists were in the corridor. The nozzle of the flame thrower, phosphorescent in the darkness, roved to and

fro, spraying roof, floor and the wall opposite . . . . Despite
the ardour which his men showed in sousing the walls and
hissing flames with the water from their buckets, Hernandez felt that all were anxiously awaiting the moment the
fascists would burst in, and the way some of them were
hugging the walls gave him an impression they did not
mean to put up much resistance . . . . As the spray crept
slowly forward the movements of the *milicianos* drenching
the walls with water grew more and more frenzied. The
hiss of steam mingled with nerve-racking coughs from
throats rasped by the pungent fumes of petrol and the
rancid sweat forming upon the nozzle. Sizzling, the shaft
of fire gained foot by foot, and sudden, sputtering bursts
of bluish flame chequered the walls with a fantastic rout
of dancing shadows as the *milicianos* turned and twisted
in their frantic saraband; it was as though a horde of phan-
toms were capering with glee around the madness of the
living men. And somehow the living forms seemed more
spectral than those wildly capering shadows, less palpable
than the stifling fog across which solid shapes showed flat
as stencils, less real than the angry hiss of fire and water
and the weak, whimpering cries of a burnt man.[69]

The flame thrower has almost reached the threshold when
the Negus, flattened against the wall and almost touched by
its nozzle, fires his revolver. The man behind it falls, "his
head bumping against the nozzle, which spluttered and flung
it off, like a foot kicking aside an obstacle."[70] The Negus
picks up the projector and points it in the opposite direc-
tion, advancing slowly with it, followed by his men. "The
corridor by which they returned was in darkness, but for a
glimmer of light from the door at the far end. The Negus
lit a cigarette; as one man the others followed his example—

[69] *Ibid.*, p. 131.
[70] *Ibid.*, p. 132.

their return to life. Each man's face showed up for a second in the brief, brisk glow of match or lighter; then the gloom closed in again."[71] When they come out, they are greeted by joyous shouts: "There's a plane up there, above the clouds."[72]

Heaven, earth, and the underworld are seen drawn into the fight in rapid alternation, and then are seen linked as Saturn's inimical spell is simultaneously confronted in all spheres and their impenetrable circles are broken open.

The other crucial tunnel episode which occurs near the end of the novel is experienced by the Republican bomber Attignies. This episode climaxes a baptism of dread that has immersed him in all four elements: air, fire, water, and earth. Flying over the mass exodus of people escaping from the Italian and Spanish bombers and mechanized columns, Attignies and his men succeed in wiping out the enemy; then they are shot down. The flaming plane plunges into the sea. Badly wounded, Attignies manages to reach shore and gets on one of the carts that are streaming by along the road, filled with fugitives and their belongings.

"Fires had been lighted in the fields; fires from which, as from those who sat or lay motionless round them, emanated the same sense of hideous suffering as from the flight itself. Between the fields, the unresisting mass of homeless humanity continued the forlorn migration to Almeria."[73] The vehicles get stuck on the road and Attignies borrows a donkey from an old peasant. On the donkey—man's timeless companion in his flight from disaster—he advances slowly,

[71] *Ibid.*
[72] *Ibid.*
[73] *Ibid.*, p. 435.

carried along by the crowd surging all around him. Suddenly
the road enters a tunnel:

> Attignies looked for his electric torch. No good taking it
> out of that soaking wet pocket. Countless little lights—
> lamps of all kinds, matches, torches, flares, were flashing
> into life and dying out, yellow or reddish; others remained
> alight, throwing out a halo, on both sides of the stream of
> humanity, beasts and earth. Protected against aeroplanes,
> a huge caravanserai of nomads had come into subterranean
> existence there, between the two far-away disks of day-
> light.[74]

An intellectual who, like Scali and a number of other heroes
in *Man's Hope,* feels at home only in the realm of ideas and
is hopelessly uprooted from the earth, Attignies feels stifled
and overcome by terror in this "fast-closed world in the
bowels of the earth."[75] He is moved along by the crowd of
peasants and by the sturdy animal.

> The daylight was getting nearer; blazing out suddenly
> as the road turned a corner, it vivified his body as if its
> rays had been ice-cold. He was amazed to find everything
> still there . . . his throbbing feet, the donkey between his
> legs. Now that he had survived both the air and the crash,
> he felt the shadows giving place once more to the mystery
> of life. Once more the tawny soil of Spain rose up around
> the flood of fugitives, as far as the Mediterranean with
> black goats standing on the rocks.[76]

Life, mysterious and indestructible, faces him suddenly,
in a succession of humble and sad, yet triumphant, images.
The doctor's car, which has picked him up with several other

[74] *Ibid.,* p. 437.
[75] *Ibid.*
[76] *Ibid.*

wounded men, stops again and picks up a peasant holding a
sick child. There is no more room inside the car and the
peasant has to sit on the fender. Holding the child in one
arm, he grips with the other the arm of one of the men
inside, to support himself. Attignies and the doctor are
strangely moved by the sight of those joined hands. They
are suddenly glimpsing, amidst all that pain and destruction
and flight, a mysterious affirmation of life, totally inaccessible
to intellectual apprehension. "Yet something fundamental in
Attignies remained linked to those hands—that same part of
him which had caused the driver to stop the car a moment
before, that which recognized maternity, childhood, and
death even in their most incongruous aspects."[77]

The next time we see a plane rise into the night, it is
just before dawn and the plane is guided in its take-off by
the same humble fires that flickered in the tunnel. A group
of peasants have gathered at the airfield and are burning
dry oranges to light the pilot's way.

> With the wind still carrying the smell of the burning
> oranges from the field, and the interior of the plane still
> in darkness, the rising sun showed up the merry, ruddy
> features of the gunner in the lower turret. "Hulloh,
> chief!" Magnin could not take his eyes off the laughter-
> widened mouth, with the broken teeth, so oddly pink in
> the first rays of the rising sun. It was getting lighter in the
> plane . . . day was breaking on the earth below.[78]

The nocturnal temperament and spirit of the Malrauvian
Magnin is sustained here in its dangerous encounter with
both the inimical sky and the enemy below at Teruel, by

77 *Ibid.*, p. 440.
78 *Ibid.*, p. 458.

the radiance of his gunner below, and the peasant by his side. "Magnin had grown used now to the primordial peace of that high world so aloof from men's restless strivings; but this time the world of men imposed itself even up there."[79] After the target's destruction, his plane returns safely to its base; but one of the companion planes is hit by enemy pursuit planes and crashes into the snowy summits of the Teruel mountains. Later, in a sublimely beautiful scene, Magnin and a group of Linares peasants are seen slowly descending the mountain, carrying the dead and wounded fliers on stretchers. It is a heroic and dangerous march, past steep gorges above which birds of prey are crying in the cold. Having struggled up the mountains, these men are now rescuing their lost brothers from the treacherous, magic heights and are bringing them back to the earth—that menaced yet resplendent earth symbolized by a gnarled apple tree and the grave faces of the peasant women.

> The steady rhythm of their tread over the long pain-burdened journey seemed to fill the vast ravine, down which the last cries still came floating from the birds above, with a solemn beat like a funeral drum. But it was not death which haunted the mountains at that moment; it was triumphant human will.[80]

The spiral linking of earth and heaven in the upward curve of the planes and the peasants' descent from the mountain is a human victory and a liberation. The last time a plane goes up in *Man's Hope*—the "Orion," one of the last, ramshackle planes that the Republican air force can still muster against the growing air power of the Fascists—we see

[79] *Ibid.*, p. 459.
[80] *Ibid.*, p. 484.

it more buffeted than ever and as ever "struggling against
the darkness closing in upon the destinies of Spain, just as
night had fallen—how long ago that seemed!—on Marcelino's homing flight."[81] But unlike Marcelino's plane, the
"Orion" returns safely, unharmed by the gathering dusk.

[81] *Ibid.,* p. 495.

III

META-
MORPHOSES

1

Mystery

Night does not fail to close in again after the plane's return, as it must in a world that is conceived as essentially nocturnal and in a time that is moving toward death. But the will of the heroes in *Man's Hope*, sustained by the hope and the patience of the people, has achieved the greatest step that the human spirit is called upon to take in periods of despair, and without which even miracles may well be inoperative: to unmask and "withstand the demonic fascination of the night"[1] and to persevere in a lucid rejection of it until an open door reveals itself at the end of the blind tunnel. The authenticity of this achievement of the will which we have seen culminating in *Man's Hope* is all the more impressive in that it is free of the exaltation of a suspect humanism found in so many "dawnist" writers.

The open door through which Malraux's heroes return from the land of death has indeed been reached by them by purely natural efforts; but this door opens out upon the counterpart of the supernatural dread induced by the closed cycle of fatality; namely, on the sense of an open world of mystery.

[1] *Les Noyers de l'Altenburg* (Paris: Gallimard, 1948), p. 250.

99

In *The Walnut Trees of Altenburg,* already the continuity of young Berger's memoirs, with their prolongation into the past—into the memoirs of the father, Vincent Berger—and into a future anticipated with a sense of rediscovery and joy, introduces us into the open reality of an "eternal present" of man, a "secret mystery" which will now in its turn furnish the answers in the dialogue with fate. What an impressive metamorphosis this continuous Malrauvian dialogue has undergone: first, the monologue of the "conqueror" novels, in which the silent nocturnal sky is heard reverberating in the world prison and again in the inner prison of the alienated human mind and imagination; then it is transformed in *Man's Fate* and *Man's Hope* into a dialogue between the heroes' will to "humanize" the world and the inimical elements, both cosmic and human; now in *The Walnut Trees,* we hear the dialogue between a "world of miracle" and a "world of fatality"[2] waged within the confines of human consciousness alone.

Under a radiant sun shining in a limpid, untroubled sky and imbuing the splendid fields of Reichbach—seat of the Altenburg—with a soft glow, questions and answers alternate in a sequence of scenes in which sun, stars, earth, and trees form but the background and symbols for the mystery and the fatality, the "secret of life" and the will-to-death that are battling in the human psyche.

In the center of the novel stands a seemingly insoluble philosophical predicament—a closed prison cell conceived by a despairing and dehumanized intellect and will to power. It is set off all around by episodes of which each becomes an open door leading to the "secret" which will defy "con-

2 *Ibid.,* p. 143.

quest" and triumph over it. The closed central prison is that of the fatalist Spenglerian circles which the German Möllberg weaves around the separate destinies of civilizations in those slightly ludicrous Altenburg colloquies the topic of which is "The Permanence and Metamorphosis of Man."

We hear human destiny discussed by a group of intellectuals who have become blind and deaf to the immediate data of human existence and the world, and who seek in vain with their dissociated and autonomously functioning minds to spin life into an intelligible, rational yarn. In this "cloister of thought,"[3] in which electric lamps are "fixed at eye level"[4] while outside the sun is glistening, Möllberg expounds his theory of the rise and fall of civilizations. Each of these, according to him, constitutes a closed entity or phenomenon of the spirit which is essentially irreconcilable with the civilizations that have preceded or followed it. The vision to be abstracted from these unrelated, even mutually exclusive cycles of history would preclude any possibility of defining a basic, unchanging human essence. It would on the contrary seem to indicate that men can be defined only, and are profoundly separated, by the particular fatalities to which their own historical moments are subject. The only possible synthesis conceivable, therefore, would be one evolved from a *dialogue postiche*[5] between these cycles after their deaths, or as Möllberg puts it, after they have been reduced from psychic realities to "sclerosed ideas."[6]

It is interesting to see how vigorously Malraux satirizes this German choking on his Hegel, who is obsessed with

3 *Ibid.*, p. 85.
4 *Ibid.*, p. 83.
5 *Ibid.*, p. 148.
6 *Ibid.*

logic and unity and in private surrounds himself with little gargoyles whom he calls "his monsters"—Hargnebouzylle, Tristophas, Hilaroblique, Malempeine—united in a "long succession of sadness."[7] He does get the better, in *The Walnut Trees of Altenburg*, of Möllberg and his fatalistic conception, which blocks all doors to a true, existential "encounter with man" because it substitutes petrified moments of civilizations for the living mystery of a concrete present. Nevertheless we will see him very nearly succumb to the same dialectical temptation in *The Voices of Silence*, as well as to the correlative temptation of overemphasizing art as will, and conqueror of a cosmic abyss.[8]

Not only the mystery of life which they fear, but also the mystery of art which they worship, escapes Möllberg and the esthetes, Walter Berger, founder of the colloquies, and Count Rabaud; and this, even though they base their whole concept of man on the data furnished by art and make of art their idol and their consolation. "Statues or logs"—that is, "civilizations or animals"[9] are the alternatives they see facing man. Between the obsessive quest for an impossible, abstract synthesis, a chemical purity of the spirit on the one hand, and the obscurity of everlasting unconscious animal life on the other, mankind seems doubly condemned: its elite, its thinkers, and artists, either to the despair caused by inescapable contradiction or to flight into alienation, and its masses to undifferentiated chaos. This Manichean separation established by Möllberg would render the genesis of art impossible, severing as it does the blossom from the root,

7 *Ibid.*, p. 105.
8 Cf. the following chapters.
9 *Les Noyers de l'Altenburg*, p. 152.

the artist from man, and turning both into two abstract concepts.

But the circle is flung open by a living miracle witnessed one day by Walter Berger and never forgotten, even though he seems not really to have understood it. The memory he relates to Vincent, his nephew, is that of the sudden, mysterious chant of a poet whose song seems to have shaken his desiccated soul and "defied the stars" precisely because it was *not* conceived in an aloof sphere of abstraction. On the contrary it is heard rising out of the poet's own precarious "present," a present steeped in the dual darkness of a long tunnel and an alienated mind; and yet, as every true present, it is pregnant with the "secret of life." Walter relates how he happened to be in Turin one day when he heard that his friend Nietzsche was in the same town and had just gone mad. He succeeded in getting the sick man on the train to take him back to Bâle. Having put Nietzsche between himself and another friend, he recalls sitting through the trip in fearful apprehension of an outburst of violence.

> The train entered the St. Gothard Tunnel, which had just been completed. In those days it took thirty-five minutes to go through—thirty-five minutes—and the carriages, the third-class ones at any rate, had no lighting. Swaying about in the dark, the smell of soot, the feeling that the journey would never end. . . . And all of a sudden —you . . . you know that several of Friedrich's works were still unpublished—a voice began to make itself heard in the darkness, above the din of the wheels. Friedrich was singing—enunciating clearly, though when he talked he used to stutter—he was singing a poem which was unknown to us; and it was his last poem, *Venice*. I don't like Friedrich's compositions. They're mediocre. But this song

. . . well, by God, it was sublime. He had stopped long
before the end of the tunnel. When we came out of the
darkness, everything was as it was before. As it was before
. . . the same wretched carriage. The same peasant girl, the
hen, the workmen, and this dentist. And ourselves, and
he, in a daze. The mystery you have just mentioned, I
have never since felt it so strongly. All this was so . . . so
accidental . . . and Friedrich was much more distressing
than a corpse. It was life—I merely say: "It was life."
Something . . . something very strange was happening:
the song was as strong as life itself. I had just discovered
something. Something important. In the prison which
Pascal describes, men manage to drag out of themselves
an answer which, if I may say so, cloaks those who are
worthy of it with immortality. And in that carriage, now,
and sometimes since—I merely say: "sometimes"—the
millenia of the starlit sky seemed as completely wiped out
by man as our own petty destinies are wiped out by the
starlit sky.[10]

The episode is moving and deeply significant, and yet
Vincent Berger cannot entirely share Walter's exhilaration
with what the esthete considers the function of art; namely,
the deliverance of privileged beings from "monsters, death,
and the gods."[11] To him art thus appropriated as an acquired
treasure seems a means of evading the existential reality of
man and the mystery of art's genesis which this reality con-
tains. To unmask the truth of man's situation is the very thing
for the sake of which Vincent has returned to Europe, after
playing for many years a "conqueror" role in the Near East.

Unlike the "conquerors" of the early novels, Berger has
returned from the actual and symbolical deserts of a legend-

10 *Ibid.*, pp. 95, 96, 97.
11 *Ibid.*, p. 77.

ridden, deceitful, and "faceless" Orient. He has returned, to rediscover in what seems at first the disconcerting absence of the Moslem veil, the naked human face, and with it the mystery of man, in the only continent in which that mystery has, since the earliest centuries, unfolded and borne fruit— "Europe with its green lands."[12] For many years, life had been to him the mere function of a myth—the myth of Enver Pasha's Young Turk movement to which he had dedicated himself.

Then, one day, he found himself suddenly and incomprehensively delivered from its spell as the result of a madman's attack on his person. Sobered by this experience and restored to his clear senses, his revolt against Europe and his own heritage brusquely terminated, he has just returned and finds himself seized by the half-anguished, half-joyous sense of rediscovering the undisguised faces of people, their laughter, their mystery. They seem still deeply rooted in that "eternal present" of the Middle Ages which, unchanging and yet pregnant with a "mysterious human freedom,"[13] is the exact opposite of the Orient's "eternal presence"[14] of fatality that he has left behind. Like a stranger from another planet, we see him, upon landing, walk through the streets of Marseilles, overwhelmed by that "anguished freedom"[15] in which human destiny is accepted not as a fate but as an adventure and a gift; as a "secret . . . not of death but of life."[16]

He remembers this first evening in Marseilles as he listens

[12] *Ibid.,* p. 70.
[13] *Ibid.,* p. 91.
[14] *Ibid.,* p. 140.
[15] *Ibid.,* p. 92.
[16] *Ibid.*

to Walter Berger. He feels forced to reject his uncle's living for and through art—his notion that human destiny is but a function of art—as he felt forced previously to reject Enver's myth and to strip his own personality of its "conqueror" or shaman quality. Obsessed now with the mystery of man which is diametrically opposed to myth and abstraction alike, to everything that tends to seal and petrify reality and to preclude its free and unpredictable movements, he is well aware that there will be no art once men cease to respect life and resort instead to living for the art forms of the past.

A poem, a sculpture, as the justification of existence—as propounded by Count Rabaud in the course of the colloquy, the "eternity of masterpieces" as proof of man's identity with himself through the ages—is the pitiful evasion of starry-eyed and secretly desperate idealists. Impatiently, and somewhat anxiously, Malraux disposes of them and that part of himself that suffers from the same nostalgic dream. He does not in the least share their equally pitiful misunderstanding of the true nature and genesis of art, or their shrinking from the reality of earth and clay from which alone a new flowering of mystery can spring, whether in the order of beauty or in the order of charity. He makes us aware that neither Möllberg's philosophical despair nor Count Rabaud's ecstatic ravings can do the least bit toward helping men to "recapture the world" in the true sense of striking roots once more in the muddy but fertile soil, so that human destiny may once more grow upon it and unfold the dual mystery of its image-making faculty and its power of love.

After the colloquy is over, Vincent walks out into the sunlit fields. As he reflects, deeply upset, about those two equally fatal pitfalls, the historian's fall into the mud of a relativism in which human life is about equal in freedom and significance to the life of the ants, and the esthete's flight into a rarefied sphere where he admits only his art treasures which "the mystery of matter doesn't touch,"[17] his eyes come to rest on some old pines and two splendid walnut trees.

> The magnificence of the venerable trees was due to their great bulk, but the strength with which the twisted branches sprang from their enormous trunks, the bursting into dark leaves of this wood which was so heavy and so old that it seemed to be digging down into the earth and not tearing itself away from it, created at the same time an impression of free will and of an endless metamorphosis.[18]

He observes

> . . . the venerable thrust of the living wood, the two sturdy, gnarled growths which dragged the strength out of the earth to display it in their boughs . . . . Instead of supporting the weight of the world, the tortured wood of these walnut trees flourished with life everlasting in their polished leaves under the sky and in their nuts that were almost ripe, in all their aged bulk above the wide circle of young sprouts and the dead nuts of winter.[19]

Uniting Möllberg's two irreconcilable poles of "statues and logs" in a living mystery, each tree seems to Berger like a "kindly statue which the strength of the earth carved for itself, and which the sun at the level of the hills spread across the sufferings of humanity as far as the horizon."[20]

[17] *Ibid.*, p. 98.
[18] *Ibid.*, p. 151.
[19] *Ibid.*, p. 152.
[20] *Ibid.*, pp. 152–53.

The trees greet Berger with the impact of an unexpected answer. Suddenly he sees before him a perfect nature symbol of human society, with its massive, unchanging populace close to the earth, and its delicate, artfully differentiated, endlessly creative elite above. By the same token each tree is a symbol of what man himself, and particularly the intellectual, potential "conqueror" or imperialist of the mind, must once again become: a being who, instead of "tearing himself away from the earth," firmly roots himself in it and in his people so that, thus solidly sustained, his imagination and his will need no longer either wither completely or give birth to monstrous and sterile blossoms.

As in *Man's Hope* we saw heaven and earth linked by the heroes' will to humanize both, to wrench them from darkness and restore them to the status of friendly powers, so we see throughout *The Walnut Trees of Altenburg* a dual movement of reconciliation being accomplished within and between men themselves. The first of these is the reconciliation, accomplished partially in Vincent Berger and then more completely in his son, between the "Gothic," anonymous character of the people and the potential "conqueror" personalities; the other and subsequent one is the gradual reconciliation of the intellect and will with that inherent "mystery" in man which is his gift of soaring past all limits of determination to "song" or silent compassion.

Before this reconciliation is accomplished, however, Malraux sets up, for the last time, the detached and demonic will of the "conquerors" and its closed sphere of doom against the open world of miracle manifest in nature herself and in the people who live in unison with the earth. The scene is that of the gas attack launched by the Germans on

the Russian front in the First World War. In this scene
which is the dramatic climax of the novel, the poison of the
same dehumanized intellect which we heard abstracting
deadly concepts from living reality in the colloquies becomes
incarnate in the poison gas. It is seen not only transforming
the sphere within its reach into a black "valley of death,"[21]
but imbuing it with so pure a "demonic presence" that to
the senses of the witness, Vincent Berger, "the Spirit of Evil
was stronger than death."[22]

The gas to be used in this attack has been invented by
Hoffmann, professor of chemistry, embodiment of that dia-
bolical mind that will reduce all life to a mathematical
formula. This demon in disguise is so totally split off from
human reality that he claims the right to destroy thousands
of men by means of a chemical formula in the name of a
"higher principle."[23] More incredible yet, he seems unable,
despite the most precise knowledge of all the symptoms of
gas poisoning, to conceive even faintly the visitation of suffering and terror that he is about to unchain.

On the morning of the attack, a throbbing radiance of
sunlight encompasses the valley—its grass, flowers, trees, and
the transparent horizon. Visibly, the exorcism of the saturnine powers from heaven and earth has been accomplished
and no demon will descend from above. Already in earlier
pages of the novel we find Vincent greeted by the "over-
whelming commonplace mystery of life"[24] under a morning
sun which had chased the stars and in which "everything

21 *Ibid.*, p. 203.
22 *Ibid.*, p. 233.
23 *Ibid.*, p. 179.
24 *Ibid.*, p. 115.

growing out of the earth was cradled in a soft radiance."[25] The demonic power operative in the gas attack episode will no longer be seen as the eruption of an outer, cosmic fatality as in the earlier "Oriental" novels; rather it is now seen as the breaking loose of one aspect of the human psyche, that fundamental reality which has, throughout its history, preoccupied the anthropocentric West. This time Malraux depicts for us a "fight to the death with death" that is waged between man's mysterious gift of affirmation and self-transcendence, and an intellect imprisoned in the closed cycle of ideas and bound to suspend life and to fix it in the image of its own deadly rigidity.

This suspense is evident, even before the bombs are released, in the still dread of anticipation of the German soldiers who are to hurl the bombs against the enemy:

My father—writes young Berger in his diary—was reminded of the town in *The Thousand and One Nights,* where every human gesture, the life of flowers, the flames of a lamp, were arrested by the Angel of Death . . . . In this mushroom-bed smell my father saw, for a split second, the petrified gestures of the mythological blacksmiths under a light forever forgotten—a light scarcely dimmed by the passage of fleeting human wills, fleeting as the war and as the German army.[26]

During those hours of suspense, Berger hears the murmuring of the soldiers, the anxious talk by which they seek to distract themselves from the obsessive thought of the gas bombs. As many years later his son will listen to the voices of the French prisoners of war in the Chartres camp, so his father

25 *Ibid.,* p. 114.
26 *Ibid.,* pp. 198–99.

now listens to the trivial exchanges of those hushed men, to that "prehistoric murmur"[27] of a race that does not seem to have changed since the *fabliaux,* since Breughel. Their talk seems common and stupid enough; their response to life is not to be found in their words. "Their love is a secret even for themselves, their friendship—an exchange of silence."[28] But between the verbal "conquerors" and these inarticulate, rude men, there is no doubt as to which side battles in behalf of death's secret, which in behalf of the secret of life. As his son will be, so Vincent is now face to face with the "fundamental substance"[29] of man which will rise up in unexpected answer to the "conquerors'" (the Germans' own officers') command.

Soon after the bombs have been released over the Russian lines, the valley is unrecognizable, a manmade hell with not a trace of life left: "Soon the bottom of the valley was only a yellow fog, reddening along the sides of the fields and the green fir-trees . . . . Slowly the sheet of gas spread out to the depth of half a mile, engulfing the valley completely."[30] "As though it had left in its wake a huge slice of winter under the radiant sky,"[31] all is black and still.

All the grass underneath the killed apple trees was black, a black never seen before. Black the trees enclosing the horizon, and slimy too; dead the woods across which some shapes of German soldiers were now moving. . . . Dead the grass, dead the leaves, dead the earth . . . .[32]

27 *Ibid.,* p. 26.
28 *Ibid.,* p. 28.
29 *Ibid.,* p. 29.
30 *Ibid.,* p. 203.
31 *Ibid.,* p. 209.
32 *Ibid.,* p. 218.

After a breathless waiting for a response from the enemy artillery which remains silent, the German infantry is ordered to move across the field over which the gas has already dispersed, to occupy the Russian lines. Again the officers, among them Berger, wait in growing suspense. The men have disappeared; no one is to be seen. Panic-stricken, Berger sets off by himself through the open, devastated field glistening now with a poisonous dew. Suddenly hundreds of strange figures become visible, tottering toward him, "fairy-ground giants." "They were made of two men in shirt sleeves, one carrying the other."[33] He fails to understand. As they come closer, he sees on their faces a delirious expression of horror and pity. In utter bewilderment he asks what all this is about, whether they have received orders to retreat. They merely look at him with contempt, without answering; some of them shout and laugh hysterically. Now he realizes that these Germans are carrying dying Russians on their shoulders. A German, with the face of an old peasant, bending under the weight of a gasping, purple-faced, writhing man, stops with a menacing gesture: "Must do something" he simply says and struggles on. Another comes toward him: "Through all this nauseating brilliance, a tiny spark of light shone out, like a window which a beam from the setting sun suddenly causes to flash out. It was shining on the chest of a soldier bent under the weight of a Russian—the double bead of the Huguenot cross."[34] In a delirium of dread, Berger fixes his eyes on this tiny cross, then in confused and broken phrases, questions the man again. Has there been an order to retreat? The German stares at him. " 'There

[33] *Ibid.*, pp. 214–15.
[34] *Ibid.*, p. 226.

aren't any orders anymore,' he said at last. Unable to make
any gesture under the heavy body he was carrying, he shook
his head as if to explain that orders had vanished forever
. . . . 'No, a man is not made to rot like that' . . . . 'If warfare
turns into that . . . .' "[35]

Berger, himself in pain now and breathing more and more
heavily, finally gets to the Russian lines. There a sight so
appalling meets his eyes that the devastated earth recedes in
comparison, becomes insignificant: bodies of hundreds upon
hundreds of Russian victims of the poison gas, their faces
distorted by unutterable agony. The annihilation of the
whole earth seems as nothing now "compared with the face
of a single gas casualty: on those stretches of ground struck
by a biblical curse my father saw only the death of men."[36]

Only now he fully understands what has prompted those
Germans to load the Russians who were not yet dead on
their shoulders and bring them back with agonizing haste:
they should have died themselves under the strain of a guilt
so overpowering, so inhuman. Gasping with horror and
growing pain but strangely delivered, he watches their "bar-
rage of pity,"[37] as they drag the still-living victims toward
the ambulances, to save them. Himself fatally gassed, he still
succeeds in dragging himself back through fields which
have remained untouched by the poison and are aglow with
life, color, and fragrance. It is like a return to the valley
of a Promised Land which symbolizes to him the mystery of
love that he has just seen. This mystery has superseded the
"conquerors' " order and, like the light and pliable straw

[35] *Ibid.,* pp. 228–29.
[36] *Ibid.,* p. 234.
[37] *Ibid.,* p. 235.

in the field, it would be an inexhaustible seed of regeneration.

> This spark that had . . . illuminated the deeps teeming
> with monsters and buried gods is . . . a mystery that would
> not yield its secret but only its presence, a presence so
> simple and absolute that it cast into nothingness all
> thought connected with it—in the same way no doubt as
> does the presence of death.[38]

Vincent dies from the effect of the poison, but the same epiphany will be re-experienced by his son and become a door to life.

> Ah, the three Magi did not bring gifts to the Infant—
> young Berger will write afterwards.—They only told him
> that on the night he was born open doors were banging in
> the dim light—doors opened on to this life which, this
> morning for the first time, has shown as powerful as the
> darkness and as powerful as death.[39]

For the first time in the work of Malraux, the link of a true, creative filiation allows the father's conquest over fate to point the way for the son. No longer is he doomed to go from nowhere to death. And this can be so because Vincent Berger's has been a true, if partial, conquest which has stripped the world of its masks of death and subsequently revealed both the fundamental image of man and that mysterious destiny of his which defeats mere speculation. His son, picking up Vincent's notes entitled "My Encounters with Man," will continue these "encounters" along the same path of rediscovery and reconciliation.

Over twenty-five years later, after Hitler's army has routed

[38] *Ibid.*, pp. 243–44.
[39] *Ibid.*, pp. 290–91.

the French, young Berger notes down in the Chartres war prisoners' camp:

> From wasted day to wasted day I am increasingly obsessed by the mystery which does not conflict with the indeterminate aspect of my companions who sing while they hold out under the infinity of the nocturnal sky. Rather does it link it up, by a long-forgotten path, with the nobility which men do not know exists in themselves, with the victorious side of the only animal that knows he has to die.[40]

It is war again. The battle now related by the son has been a tank battle between the French and the Germans in the fields of Flanders. It does not matter, for, as young Berger's notes tell us, "The enemy is not the German, it is track breaking, the mine and the anti-tank ditch."[41] Whereas the father was still halfway on the side of the "conquerors" or at least an observer standing equally apart from the intellectuals and the people, we now see the son engaged in the battle in an outfit in which he is most likely the only man who has ever heard of philosophy. But he is one with these men, united with them in their common battle and on a "single cross."[42] To them, the protagonists of this battle are not the French fighting the Germans; they are living men fighting the deadly abstractions of the mind that turn both men and the earth into specters of dread. There are no more harvest fields, "There are only fields of ditches, fields of mines."[43] The whole world seems to have become "a world of ditches."[44]

40 *Ibid.*, p. 250.
41 *Ibid.*, p. 268.
42 *Ibid.*, p. 281.
43 *Ibid.*, p. 269.
44 *Ibid.*

With "sad fortitude," the peasant's age-old determination in the face of a scourge, the three other men in Berger's tank and himself set out toward the battle scene. "Nothing to do but to follow this road in the night and come closer and closer to the war."[45] This fortitude is not so much a will as it is a patience, the timeless patience of men who know that life always goes on and that scourges pass, and whose instinctive sense of continuity and duration enables them to "wait for it to wear off."[46]

The tank moves over the fields in utter darkness. Suddenly they feel themselves "sliding in panic on a surface which gives way."[47] Have they fallen into an anti-tank ditch? "One does not get out of a ditch."[48] Minutes of agony in which they know that they are lost, that death has come for them, that any second the inevitable anti-tank gun pointed at every anti-tank ditch will go off. There is no sound; derisively, above the pitchblack darkness of the ditch onto which the door of the tank has opened, a patch of sky shines through between the camouflage tree trunks. They are trapped below and above. "It is as if we were in those dungeons where daylight only comes in through an inaccessible trap door; prisoners cannot escape through the roof."[49] But, miracle, they do. Suddenly the tracks catch hold of the treacherous ground, the tank slowly moves upward and pushes its way through the heavy trunks. Counter to all mathematics, to all reckoning, even the most demonic fatality is proven fallible; they are freed, back on the road.

[45] *Ibid.*, p. 252.
[46] *Ibid.*, p. 26.
[47] *Ibid.*, p. 273.
[48] *Ibid.*, p. 275.
[49] *Ibid.*, p. 282.

Once again, a Berger is before the unpredictable mystery of the open door. Already, as they now drive through the night, "the darkness which is no longer the tomb of the ditch, the living darkness appears to me like a prodigious gift."[50]

When he awakens the next morning, with his companions, in a barn in the next little village which the Germans have already evacuated, Berger is overwhelmed by the morning's loveliness. "Now from that night there rises the miraculous revelation of day."[51] Resurrected from a dread tomb and looking, as if for the first time and through the eyes of a stranger, at the "old and so stubborn life"[52] and at its myriad and wondrous signs—all taking their places in the world of man—he feels himself "in the presence of an unaccountable gift, an apparition. All this might never have been, might never have been as it is."[53] He is scarcely able "to remember what fear is like."[54] An old peasant couple is sitting on a bench, worn and stooped by hardship and age. "Yet she smiles, a slow, pensive, delayed smile . . . she seems to be viewing death at a distance, with patience and even— oh the mystery of those fluttering eyelids, the sharp shadows in the corner of her eyes!—even with irony."[55]

[50] *Ibid.*, p. 284.
[51] *Ibid.*, p. 290.
[52] *Ibid.*, p. 288.
[53] *Ibid.*
[54] *Ibid.*, p. 292.
[55] *Ibid.*, p. 291.

2

The Stripping of Masks

Death, where is thy sting? the old woman's smile seems
to say as, for a fleeting moment, its power wrenches
the earth from "the awe-inspiring realm of the
Mothers."[56]

After the lucid and tenacious journey which Malraux's
characters have pursued, that almost imperceptible curving
of the old woman's lips at the end of *The Walnut Trees of
Altenburg* symbolizes a reconciliation: for a moment the
earth is restored to man's dominion and the hero's sense
of dread and rebellion is resolved into harmony and acceptance. For a moment the stars are eclipsed, or rather, have
"ceased being a fatality"[57] and come to revolve within the
orbit of man's world. The hero's will to conquer and
possess the demonic forces which have masked and estranged
from him heaven, earth, and his own self, and sought to
make him a blind prisoner, has given way to a mysterious

[56] "Museum without Walls," *The Voices of Silence*, trans. Stuart Gilbert
(Garden City: Doubleday, 1953), p. 81.

[57] "Le Musée Imaginaire," *Les Voix du Silence* (Paris: Galerie de la Pléiade,
NRF, 1951), p. 79. This is my own translation. I shall quote from the original
wherever I feel that Stuart Gilbert's version either slightly deviates from the
original or weakens a thought or a key word.

realization of freedom and of harmony with the cosmos.

This ephemeral moment of reconciliation crowns a sustained and painful quest which, throughout the novels, has defined itself negatively as a confronting, unmasking, and repudiating of the demonic aspects of the contemporary scene. On the level of time and situation, victory has throughout been seen as remaining on the side of the "tireless orchestra of death."[58] But Malraux's relentless attack on illusion and sentimentality, his merciless uncovering of the myths and falsehoods through which this civilization has been disguising its growing inner and outer terror, constitutes in itself a conquest and a source of hope. For, as the novels signify, unless our time can fearlessly elucidate its destiny and face up to the threats which press in on it from all sides, it is doomed not merely to move but to race toward death.

Both on the level of poetic realization embodied in the novels' movement and images, and on the level of the heroes' existential realization of a human "quality" that summons man to strip the world of appearances of its false autonomy and re-establish his power of holding discourse with the gods, fate's dominion has been destroyed. This discourse alone, whether accusing or affirming, guarantees man's liberation from dread. It represents, on man's side, an act of "humanizing" the otherwise wholly incommensurate; that is, of rendering it accessible to his experience and thereby transforming its power from that of a crushing "fascination" into that of a liberating "mystery" or presence.

The continuous dialogue that Malraux succeeds in establishing between the demoniac in contemporary man and

[58] "Aftermath of the Absolute," *The Voices of Silence*, p. 631.

his world and a transcendent reality which has taken on the negative value of an absence and become a source of anguish and obsession, is a powerful realization in negative form of an act of faith. It is a tragic realization born out of a sense of the absolute which allows of no direct positive expression. Heir of the nineteenth-century traditions of metaphysical rebellion and German historical philosophy, and searching prophet of his own overtly agnostic generation, Malraux cannot but leave the language of faith in the tomb and focus his vision on preparing its resurrection. His Christian heritage in full process of dissolution, its theocentric structure and inner cohesion crumbling away since the Renaissance, the reality in terms of and beyond which he is forced to conceive the absolute is a pluralism of values, an endless multiplicity of events and, in the realm of speculative thought, the substitution of history and "becoming" for a theology of "being." The love preached on the Mount, which for centuries was recognized by men in the incarnate presence of God in the world and which wrenched them from the clutches of death, has seemingly ceased to deliver man in our time.

> What Christian culture was discarding was . . . something even more vital than a faith; it was the notion of man orientated towards Being—who was soon to be replaced by the man capable of being swayed by ideas and acts; value was being disintegrated into a plurality of values. What was disappearing from the Western world was the Absolute.[59]

Malraux sees the fundamental predicament of our time in its loss of a sense of the absolute. For if man does not

[59] *Ibid.*, p. 481.

direct himself to an absolute value or "totality," he will succumb to false gods. The multiple demonic powers that seek to disinherit him of himself and the world will lead him to abdicate the calling on which his entire destiny hinges; namely, the calling to liberate and affirm the truth in a continuous creative act of religious faith or the formal fashioning of truth's image.

The presence of the absolute has indeed been waning from the scene; but instead of disappearing completely, as it seemed in the nineteenth century that it would, it has reappeared in our time to a number of artists and thinkers, transformed into its negative: an absence that has a powerful reality of its own. The anxiety felt, that Kierkegaardian anguish translated into agnostic terms, is directly related to the core of Malraux's works of fiction.

A transcendent "superreality" or mystery is the invisible focal point in each of the novels, upon which every essential action tends to converge. Except for *The Walnut Trees of Altenburg*, this "superreality" is consciously rendered in the negative form of an absence. A few typical examples of this (to recapitulate preceding analyses) would be Perken's painful awareness of the loss and absence of love in the course of his erotic exploits; Clappique's compulsive flight into "nonbeing" so that he does not have to face "being"; or Manuel's deep sense of discrepancy and discord between himself and his situation which, in the light of his achievements, would seem incomprehensible to an "orthodox" revolutionary serving the cause. This negative focal point is—like negative space, shadows, silences in authentic art—a powerful creative means in Malraux's hands. Through it he renders that quality or value which he cannot create positively, since it belongs to the pole opposite from that of his own *génie maudit* and comes into his heroes' orbit of vision only at the extreme point of the curve which the novels have traced; nor can he define it positively—except when, speaking of the Middle Ages, for example, he borrows the terminology of faith—because it eludes the deterministic modes of contemporary thinking, as Möllberg has shown.

Furthermore, whereas faith implies an inner repose because a central reality structures all things from within, and reference to it is possible from all spheres of human experience, Malraux's sense of alienation and his anguished quest to rediscover an abiding meaning necessarily implies the opposite: reliance on action. In default of a definable absolute, the stress is seen placed on the struggle which alone can render this absolute accessible; namely the struggle against the demons that hold man's destiny captive, and blind it with delusions, appearances, and servitudes. Only when the task of repudiation is accomplished, will man be free to possess and affirm the mystery that reconciles him to the cosmos; absence will be transformed into presence, the blindly-fought-for will reveal itself in an unpredictable form.

In no realm of action is this struggle more purely realized and this hope more gloriously crowned than in art. The long and profoundly moving dialogue which for almost twenty-five years (since 1935) Malraux has recorded, as it were, between the gigantic "presence" of the resurrected masterpieces contained in his Imaginary Museum and the annihilating voice of death, reveals not only man's triumphant conquests of meaning in the past. It also provides Malraux with a basis, beyond and parallel to that furnished by his own human and artistic experience, for defining both the essential nature of the creative act or conquest, and of the "inaccessible totality" to which each separate master-piece is a specific response and of which each is a partial incarnation. It is the first of these definitions that most likely constitutes the real value of *The Voices of Silence*. The second will be shown to be more problematic.

Malraux frankly searches, in his investigation of art, for a *summa* that might replace the great theological system that sustained the West for centuries and from which our culture is by now almost totally severed. The extreme opposite of the early Renaissance at its spiritual height—possibly the greatest moment of harmony in history, not only between the human and the divine but also between man and a world in full splendor—the present is a time in which the artist is virtually forced to repudiate the world in its entirety be-cause it is so utterly debased by its false values and its in-ferior image of man. He finds himself in such conflict with its steadily growing demand for pleasure, its material greed, its slavish worship of appearances and, in the absence of any authentic spirituality, its reveling in the deeps of the uncon-scious, that he has abandoned it to its own fate and chosen to serve and realize his own absolute.

Unable to share a single essential value with his culture, he has said an unconditional "no" to it and begun to con-ceive of art as a "totally different" world, unrelated to the "reality of appearances" except negatively by his fierce re-jection of it. Malraux points to the dangers besetting the contemporary artist's path and his creative work: as never before, art, severed both from faith and from the world, now evolves in a void and is becoming its own end and its own redemption from chaos. It is a perilous adventure. Like the hero in the dark who clearly discerns only the falsehood and dread he is withstanding but does not yet know the face of the truth for the sake of which he fights, and which will or will not emerge, so the artist makes a wager on which he stakes the meaning of his life—his faith in art. It is a wager against death.

But, miraculously, no sooner had modern art delivered the *coup de grâce* to the myth that art meant representation of the world and its idealization in terms of an "eternal divine beauty" discovered by the Greeks and to be perpetuated forever, no sooner had it broken with naturalism and sentimental "fiction," than its own agonizing solitary "inquiry" or experimentation with pure formal values called forth an unprecedented resurrection. Eastern and Western, primitive and prehistoric art forms, recent or long forgotten, responded to its appeal and suddenly revealed anew their power and meaning. Without itself having arrived at a major positive style or testimony of truth, contemporary art, by its mere vigorous rejection of a tradition of representation that had become void of all significance, has summoned back into life every great art, no matter how seemingly incongruous its style, that has upheld a transcendent, sacred reality against the world of appearances. A *summa* does in fact reveal itself to the attentive spectator who contemplates the almost infinite "metamorphoses of Apollo" in the Imaginary Museum. It is not theological and does not speak of an eternal unchanging being. But as art was never divorced from the sacred until after the Renaissance, but on the contrary has through the ages shaped, in forms of abiding life, man's personal attitude to his gods, the Imaginary Museum becomes for Malraux the only true church of our time.

All the styles that our time has resurrected, from primitive fetishes to the great Gothic cathedrals, reveal aspects of man's experience of an absolute reality which ranges from the immobile submission of the Egyptians to their gods to the Greeks' humanizing of theirs; from the dread of primitive tribes to the glowing affirmation of the god-man by the *trecento*. Periods of discord and periods of reconciliation alike have left testimonies which, mysteriously reawakened after a sleep of centuries, now hold a dialogue with one another in the consciousness of the modern artist in search of his soul.

Malraux pays tribute to all, but his most passionate analyses are those devoted to the solitary giants of the last four centuries who, out of their violent conflict with a growingly secular society, and an anguish that would "transform a bouquet of flowers into a burning bush," [60] created works that stripped the world of its complacency and its seduction and imperiously placed it in the presence of the divine or under the star of Saturn. Among the masters who draw the greatest crowds to the museums today are Rembrandt, El Greco, Goya, Van Gogh. And it is they who reveal most obviously art's fundamental aspect of rebellion and "rectification."

Malraux's analysis of El Greco and his conquest of a "Christian style" which evolved out of one of the worldliest styles the world had ever known (that of his master, Titian), is most illuminating. It reveals not only the artist's supreme freedom from the world of appearances, which to him is but an infinite sphere of possibilities from which he chooses what he needs to realize the vision that will conquer and

60 "La Création Artistique," *Les Voix du Silence*, p. 433.

"transform the world"; it also illustrates how much every genius, before he will speak with his own voice, is a prisoner of a previous style. If art is essentially rebellion against appearance and against a partial vision of the truth in the name of Truth, this rebellion takes the specific form of a battle against a style. The nonartist begins on the course toward his destiny as a "prisoner of the world," and he wages his fight against the world and in terms of a "worldly" situation. The artist begins his career as a prisoner of the style which he finds in power. And he sets out to overcome it both to free himself of its authority over him and through this struggle for liberation to come into possession of his own vision, as well as to furnish with this vision the response called for by the ever changing face of the gods.

The terms that Malraux uses to define the creative act are negative: "discontent," "refusal," "break," "destruction," "conquest," "annexation." This bears out once more the negative approach, so typical of him (and many contemporary artists), to the mystery of the absolute. In a convincing and splendidly illustrated exposition he shows that every great master's response has throughout the ages manifested itself in the "destruction" or breaking down of a formal "system of meaning." That this apparently negative process is in fact a profoundly positive response is borne out by the evidence: it is not that meaning is destroyed; only the proud autonomy of the system, its claim to totality, is revealed as false in the light of a new partial realization. For every style which, unchallenged, reigns past the period of its vital "testimony" becomes falsehood and hence a powerful weapon in the hands of fate. When it is "destroyed" by its heir and enemy, it goes into the tomb of oblivion or estrangement and awaits there its resurrection. The Imaginary Museum is vibrant with the mysterious life of forms, each of which expresses a patiently conquered relation of an aspect of man with an aspect of the sacred. Each represents a conquest over death which no other human conquest, save the saint's, can match, for it lives on past its age in a duration which is not eternity, yet defies death's power of final obliteration.

In the world, the rebel's fate is almost by necessity a tragic one. He either fails to "deliver" his truth altogether, or "delivers" it in so contaminated a form that it has itself become a falsehood; or he succeeds in imposing it on the world at the cost of being himself destroyed in the process—either physically, or, more tragically yet, by having caught his enemy's disease. But art is not of this world. As Malraux carefully elaborates, it is not conditioned in any way save by its own nature and laws; not by history, not by sociology, economy, biology, or psychology. Whatever it may reveal of any of these determinants of human life, it is not subject to them. In an ironical passage in which he points out the utter irrelevance of the vulture discovered by Freud in Leonardo's "Saint Anne," that is, its irrelevance to an understanding of the painting, Malraux sums up art's elusive and imperious freedom: "as for secrets [he refers to psychological undercurrents] and conditioning factors, they become meaningless at the point where art begins: at quality."[61] And only because art belongs to the realm of quality, is it given to the artist to destroy the masks of death without destroying in the same process either a living value or his own being. On the contrary, only by conquering the style that has preceded him can he discover his own. Only the ceaseless libera-

61 *Ibid.*, p. 418.

tion of the truth from a style which has no sooner given it life than it tends to imprison it in its autonomous empire can safeguard the truth against death's encroachment and assure its continued metamorphosis.

This vision of the creative process in art concurs very closely with Malraux's vision of human destiny. Both are conceived as movement, as a continuous process from imprisonment to freedom, from deception to mystery, from estrangement to reconciliation. We have already seen his vision of human destiny shape itself in the course of the novels where it imposes itself with a powerful immediacy. In *The Voices of Silence* it does the same, except that in the parts where Malraux translates it into a philosophical concept, its unresolved ambiguities become apparent. Where, one asks oneself, does man end and the sacred begin? Is every reality not only *in* flux but itself flux? And is there or is there not a finality? The novels and the major parts of *The Voices of Silence* strongly intimate a spiritual dynamics that seems to head toward a fulfillment, yet Malraux rejects finality on the level of discourse.

The two images that alternately express his vision of human destiny in *The Voices of Silence* do not clear up the contradictions; they even re-enforce them. But if viewed side by side, one corresponds unmistakably to Malraux's genius on its deep level of poetic intuition; the other is self-contradictory and unconvincing. The first image is that of two revolving planets—the human and the sacred—in continuous dialogue. In this dialogue fate triumphs when the human fails to give an adequate response, to discover its own relation to the sacred, and as a result is overpowered and "annexed" by it, either overtly as in the sacred cultures of the

Orient, or secretly, as in our own culture in which the demoniac is besieging the human psyche from within. Conversely, the human triumphs every time that man "humanizes" the sacred, that is, draws it into the orbit of his own experience.

The second image is that of a movement out of the void. This movement, according to an intrinsic dialectic of conflict and reconciliation, evolves truth in a continuous, even though not necessarily unilinear, blossoming forth of incarnations. Each of these is seen as a conquest over an abyss, upholding and opposing an unending metamorphosis of meaning to time's race toward death, each leaving "a scar on the path of fate."[62] This much more intellectual image compounded of a mixture of Hegelian *Weltgeist* and Heideggers' existence-unto-death seems strangely inauthentic and makes one aware that *The Voices of Silence* actually moves on two mutually contradictory levels: the level of Malraux's existential grasp and poetic realization of man's or the artist's destiny, and the level of his intellectual argument.

The image of the self-sustaining movement clashes with the basic intuition that underlies his entire work; namely, that the "mystery of man" is intimately tied up with a transcendent or sacred reality; that human destiny realizes itself not in terms of an autonomous dialectical process but in terms of an essential, if ever changing, relationship to "another world." This intuition applies equally to art. Side by side with philosophical assertions of art's absolute autonomy, according to which a painting's significance and power of presence would be determined by the quality of its pic-

[62] "Le Musée Imaginaire," *Les Voix du Silence,* p. 44.

torial relationships alone, Malraux invites us to an exposition of art as a "dialogue with fate" which in its power and
persuasiveness makes his metaphysics seem hard-pressed.

Like a revolving planet itself, the Imaginary Museum
reveals to the spectator one after another the great styles of
the past which men have evolved in response to a transcendent reality that has not ceased to revolve and change according to a "mysterious rhythm," showing now a benign and
now a terrible face, emanating by turns a divine radiance,
a magical spell, or the pale glimmer of infinite aloofness.
To each of these "metamorphoses of Apollo," art—in supreme evidence of man's infinite power of response—has
brought forth images in affirmation or accusation and, once,
a reconciliation so complete that the human and the divine
became indistinguishable from one another in their perfect
union. But in each case this very power of response incarnate in a style has liberated man from what might have been
a spell, by relating an aspect of the "other world" to an
"evident or mysterious, yet abiding human quality."[63]

Art's power of liberation becomes most obvious in a style
of accusation; Goya's for example. Conceived in a spiritual
desert by a genius who knew himself separated both from
the face of God and from his own cruel and flippant age, it
strips the world of its deceitful glitter and, by its ominous
power of exorcism, establishes a piercing dialogue between
man and the spirit of evil. "He introduces the infernal into
the world of man,"[64] Malraux says. "*Saturn* is at the same
time the other world and our own suddenly proliferating

[63] "La Création Artistique," *Les Voix du Silence,* p. 458.
[64] *Saturne: Essai sur Goya* (1st edn.; Paris: Galerie de la Pléiade, NRF,
1950), p. 110.

world—our nocturnal world lit up by the reflection of a dead planet."[65] A relation is established here between horror and the sacred, in which the demoniac is annexed to the domain of human experience and man is delivered from its fascination.

Halfway between this *art maudit* at one pole and an art of reconciliation and harmony at the other, Romanesque and early Gothic sculpture reveal to the contemporary spectator one of the profoundest discoveries art ever made: an image of the human soul itself serving as the actual battlefield on which the divine and the satanic fight for the possession of man and his world. This discovery was art's response, evolved after almost a thousand years of Christianity, to the mystery of the Incarnation. Having finally stripped the human face both of the idealization imposed upon it by Greece and of the rigid mask it was given by the highly symbolical sacred style of Byzantine art, these sculptures are the first in the whole history of art to reveal it undisguised and truly expressive. The face becomes an incarnation of the drama of man: of his struggle for redemption.

> The early Romanesque seeks out the head; and the Gothic the face; the body in Romanesque art is the symbol of all that compels man to overcome his weird and threatened condition, and the artist wrenched from it a testimony of God's transcendence. But soon afterwards, the sculptor began to substitute for the symbol of lips drawn wide apart something which had hardly counted until then: the expressive line which separates the lips. Gothic art begins at tears. For from the moment of the first composition in which the mediating Presence had made its appearance, every sculptor strove obscurely to express it

65 *Ibid.*, p. 137.

in every line of every face. Throughout the Christian
world, Gothic . . . became an Incarnation.[66]

Each face shares in the suffering of Christ and expresses the
burden of man's battle against his own demons; and "the
hands of Christ, wounded ever anew by man's very nature,
express the anguish and the pity which were born together
with the individualization of man's fate."[67]

When hope won out over anguish in the statuary of the
thirteenth century, a smile appeared on the face of the angel
of Rheims. It ushered in an art of "paradise" and reconciliation which was to include not only man himself but also
a radiant world of which he emerged as the master.

> From Chartres to Rheims and from Rheims to Assisi—in
> every land where, under the Mediator's outspread hands
> a world of seedtime and harvest . . . was permeating
> human lives (where until now there had been room for
> God alone)—in every land artists were discovering the
> forms of a world released from fear.[68]

First man alone is seen emerging from the hell and purga-
tory of Romanesque and Gothic sculpture, delivered from
his monsters and humbly proud of "the honor of being a
man."[69] The human figure found in Giotto's paintings bears
the character of a sage. "In Giotto's art man has regained the
old self-mastery of the Roman but without his pride."[70]
For the first time an artist's faith "gave every Christian his
due of majesty."[71] With Raphael, the Florentine paradise

[66] "Les Métamorphoses d'Apollon," *Les Voix du Silence,* p. 237.
[67] *Ibid.,* p. 215.
[68] "Museum without Walls," *The Voices of Silence,* p. 87.
[69] "The Metamorphoses of Apollo," *The Voices of Silence,* p. 268.
[70] *Ibid.,* p. 267.
[71] *Ibid.*

reaches its height. Man is delivered from his sorrow and the world is delivered from the demons which medieval art had seen lurking in all corners. All is reconciled to the divine in an art of serene joy in which feminine beauty, dethroned for centuries after the vanishing of the Greek "Victories" and of Venus, is fully restored to pre-eminence by the power of the Virgin.

An immense realm of dialogue and reconciliation unfolds before the spectator's eyes, as one incarnation after another tells of man's conquest of truth through forms. In this realm, surrounded by a margin of silence, there is a continuous dialogue between Apollo and Saturn, freed of all stridency and accompanied by the dialogue of styles which bear a positive affinity to one another. In mutual recognition and illumination, Goya salutes Rembrandt and Michelangelo; and Raphael's "Virgin with the Chair" fuses her radiance with that of the Smile of Rheims and the "Koré of Euthydikos."

Each style has stripped the "other world" of its autonomy, and the world of its masks. All together they constitute a *summa* of human genius and the continuous liberation of a mystery from time's deadly race. Malraux defines posterity as "the gratitude of coming generations for victories which seem to promise them their own."[72] Above this *summa* one likes to imagine standing, as at the top of the Louvre's stairway, one of the Greek "Victories"—those lovely images full of grace and movement that symbolize man's liberation.

[72] "The Creative Process," *The Voices of Silence,* p. 464.

3

The Struggle with the Angel

The Imaginary Museum, with its *summa* of styles and significances, confronts Malraux and the contemporary mind not only with an abundant affirmation of art's power of transcendence and liberation; it also places him straight before his own two-faced black angel or demon and forces him to battle. In "Museum without Walls" and "Aftermath of the Absolute" we see an angelic temptation to sever and abstract the reality of man and his "divine power" of creation from all bonds with the world of existence, and to relegate the latter entirely to the domain of death's kingdom. The sense of disdain that Malraux manifests toward a world that is experienced both as chaos and as a deceptive trap to lure the imagination away from its pursuit or conquest of the absolute strongly recalls the "conqueror" novels. And so does the other aspect of his demon; namely a "will to omnipotence" that seeks to sever art in its turn from any transcendent reality and to assert for it an unbounded freedom of creation and an absolute autonomy of meaning.

A dialogue, or rather a conflict, is apparent throughout *The Voices of Silence.* We see Malraux torn between this dual temptation which offers him a mask to conceal the void to which (he explicitly states) he and his generation are exposed—and which alternately attracts and repels him; and the virile attempt to counter the "fascination" of the void and the desire to dance on a philosophical tightrope, by rigorously focusing attention on the specific element of "fatality" inherent in every style of the past and on the specific "fatality" confronting the contemporary artist.

The Voices of Silence is Malraux's own *summa* in more than one way. It is not only his major work of poetic vision; it also recapitulates the intrinsic battle pursued in the course of the novels, between the "conqueror's" need to obliterate the world which he sees as a hateful screen between himself and the face of the absolute, and the artist's endeavor to reconquer the world and accept it as the indispensable realm of mediation between man and the absolute. By "world" is meant the realm of the specific and the time-bound, the realm of the artist's "condition," in which he encounters his own individual "fatality" or that of his time and in which he evolves his dialogue and establishes a "new system of relations between things." [73]

In every one of his luminously penetrating analyses of specific styles—whether they are Egyptian statuary, Gothic sculptures, Gallic coins, or paintings by Van Gogh—Malraux reveals the essential nature of art to be that of a response. Every great style at its height represents the "patiently elaborated expression by the artist of his fundamental experience of the universe," [74] which in its directness and power and its inner structural coherence constitutes a totality. He

[73] "Museum without Walls," *The Voices of Silence,* p. 63.
[74] "La Création Artistique," *Les Voix du Silence,* p. 412.

points out that at no time up to 1600 does the history of art reveal a major style that did not establish a relation to an aspect of the absolute—divine, saturnine, or cosmic—and that did not incarnate an exclusive vision of another world to which art served, in the eyes of the artist, as a means of access. "How could that rigid frontal pose have been discovered by an artist foreign to the values of Egypt, or the Gothic incarnation by artists knowing nothing of Christian values?"[75] A Gothic crucifix is an object; it is a sculpture but it is also a crucifix. Its sculptor did not conceive it, could not have conceived it as an abstraction, a value-in-itself, even though he conceived it by artistic means of which he was the absolute master.

In each of Malraux's analyses we see an artist's freedom, consisting in his possession of his means, encounter the fatality of his spiritual situation; and out of this encounter is born the mysterious presence of a style.

This mystery is nowhere more clearly in evidence than in the aloofness from time and contingencies of the Imaginary Museum or even the actual museums of our time. When the anguished spectator Malraux, in search of a "key," faces an immense imaginary room filled with the works of a master who speaks to him—and how many voices call out to him!—that "closed universe" opens and reveals a presence, a power of transfiguration that reaches to the depths of darkness. For "the wings of *The Victory of Samothrace* did not merely implement its triumphant line; they had been the wings of the sphinxes and harpies and were, later, to be those of angels."[76]

[75] "Aftermath of the Absolute," *The Voices of Silence,* p. 615.
[76] *Ibid.,* p. 590.

But suddenly we see the "conqueror" take over. In a development which is totally different in tone, Malraux transforms his Imaginary Museum into a fascinating no-man's land or spiritual vacuum. The specific search of the *summa* for a key that will unlock the contemporary existential and artistic stalemate is replaced and covered, as it were, by a detached intellectual atmosphere of inquiry and total *disponibilité*. Now a strange metamorphosis is produced in the works as they are admitted into a multi-focal, one-dimensional field of vision and placed side by side, stripped of their aspect of "fatality," "delivered of their matter," to hold a "dialogue of forms."

"What common link existed between a Venus which *was* Venus, a Crucifix which *was* Christ crucified, and a bust. But three 'statues' can be linked together."[77] By means of an intellectual process of reduction, each work is severed from its spiritual and existential context and the ensuing *summa* of pure forms searched in order that it might reveal an underlying common factor or value. A stained-glass window removed from its cathedral, Persian miniatures, frescoes, details of paintings, Greek vases, sculptures—the intellectual vision focuses on all forms as it seeks to relate them in terms of movement, line and color relationships, and the intrinsic significance of these. The extraordinary relevance of this *rapprochement* of styles to a true understanding of the life of forms is brilliantly shown by Malraux. There can be no doubt that this "deliverance" of styles from the specific moment of their genesis has illuminated in an unprecedented way their virtually unfathomable mystery. There is no false exaltation when he attributes a divine quality to

77 "Museum without Walls," *The Voices of Silence*, p. 53.

them, or when he places the Christians of Gothic statuary above the living sinners of the thirteenth century for purity and expressiveness. (Though this begins to be problematic.)

But from there Malraux proceeds to a further and literally fabulous abstraction. First, he chooses to forget about the specific mystery of art's genesis altogether, even though he has just warned the spectator to beware of the Museum's reductive metamorphosis which suppresses it:

> The association in our culture of very different types of art is rendered feasible only by the metamorphosis that the works of the past have undergone, not merely through the ravages of time but also because they are detached from certain elements of what they once expressed: their poetry no less than the faith of their makers and the hope of enabling man to commune with the cosmos or the dark demonic powers . . . . The Gothic world was a present reality, not a phase of history; once we replace faith by love of art, little does it matter if a cathedral chapel is reconstituted in a museum . . . for we have begun by converting our cathedrals into museums. Could we bring ourselves to feel what the first spectators of an Egyptian statue, or a Romanesque crucifixion, felt, we would make haste to remove them from the Louvre. True, we are trying more and more to gauge the feelings of those first spectators, but without forgetting our own, and we can be contented all the more easily with the mere knowledge of the former, without experiencing them, because all we wish to do is to put this knowledge to the service of the work of art.[78]

In "Aftermath of the Absolute" we now read this:

> Though we know that behind a Khmer head lie centuries of Buddhism, we look at it as if its spirituality and

[78] *Ibid.*, p. 65.

complexity must have been the invention of its maker. It conveys to us a "relativized absolute." In short, we look at great works of the remote past—whether their purport be cosmic, magical, religious, or transcendental—as so many Zarathustras invented by so many Nietzsches.[79]

Forgetting what he has made so absolutely clear, namely that until contemporary art very unhappily became its own absolute, every authentic style represented an artist's or a whole civilization's specific response to an "other world" which is by no means hypothetical, Malraux begins to construct a superart out of his Zarathustras. Suddenly, the Museum's elimination of the pole of fatality from art's dialogue has become the source of an illumination and a virtue; namely, the stripping away of a mask that has concealed art's true essence and now allows a purified vision of it. And this reveals the principle of conquest—ultimate residuum of the Museum's filtering process. In the new light, what was the artist's power of response is seen as a purely demiurgic power of creation or "conquest over chaos."[80] The entire meaning of the terminology of conquest is metamorphosed: conquest of means has become conquest as meaning; autonomy of style has become art's sovereignty over the universe of men and gods, an imperious monologue with itself. Transformation of the world is superseded by pure "invention" of a "totally other" universe, "rivalling" the world of creation. In this vision, the reality of the sacred world as well as the world of men is reduced to unreality beside the reality of forms. In the light of the steadily paling faces of the gods in our culture, Malraux's philosophy of art metamorphoses

79 "Aftermath of the Absolute," *The Voices of Silence,* p. 619.
80 "La Monnaie de l'absolu," *Les Voix du Silence,* p. 618.

art's immemorial power of mediation between the human and the sacred into demiurgy: its own bringing forth of archetypes.

> The art of Greece is for us the true god of Greece. This god it is and not the rulers of Olympus, who shows us Greece under her noblest aspect, victorious over time and near to us even today, for it is through her art alone that Greece invokes our love. Greek art stands for what was once, by way of Hellas and inseparable from her, a special manifestation of that divine power to which all art bears witness. That power has taken many forms, but all alike reveal man as protagonist in the greatest of all dramas and also the undying root whence thrust up the growths of creation, now mingling, now in isolation. . . . From the *Birth of Aphrodite* to Goya's *Saturn*, and to the Aztec crystal skulls, the radiant or tragic archetypes he has begotten tell of sudden stirrings in the deep yet restless sleep of that eternal element in Man which lies beneath the conscious threshold, and each of these voices tells of a human power sometimes exercised, sometimes in abeyance, and often lost.[81]

As if to conceal his anguish over the immediate concern that touches him, namely the precarious state of both contemporary art and the contemporary human condition, Malraux seeks to shift his vision to a level of generalization and abstraction and on this level to transform a negative into an ultimate. The real hardship, art's present lack of a positive point of reference outside itself, is seen on this plane as the ultimately purified manifestation of the fundamental and unbounded autonomy suggested by the "super-artists"[82] of the Imaginary Museum. A faulty "totalitarian" *summa* of

[81] "Aftermath of the Absolute," *The Voices of Silence*, pp. 636–37.
[82] "Museum without Walls," *The Voices of Silence*, p. 46.

art, telescoping all creative achievement throughout the ages into a false superreality of "Man," is devised to prevail against a real sense of imprisonment and loss of relation.

But Malraux never remains for long on this superstructural level; he persistently returns to the existential situation. Hegel's philosophy of history on which his own philosophy of art is so closely modeled serves him as a warning. He shows how it has led to a replacement of the totality that was inherent in all theocentric cultures of the past by the totalitarian states of the twentieth century. A true totality is by its very nature exclusive—he gives the Middle Ages as an example—but it is not totalitarian because it imposes itself by self-evidence. A totalitarian creation, to the contrary, has to impose itself by force. Whereas the first is an organism that evolves in reference to a vital value that both transcends it and also defines its limits of expression and its inner hierarchy of values, the totalitarian superstructure is basically one-dimensional and unbounded and tends toward limitless expansion.

Similarly, art which through the dislocation of a liberating value has tended to lose its power of dialogue and become its own end, is now seen as endangered in two ways: it is tempted on the one hand by the "will-to-godhead" of individualist rebellion, or, on the other, it is harnessed into the service of a state cult (as in Soviet Russia) and reduced to servile representation. In either case, it must lose its essential power of presence; that is, its power of "rectifying the world" by transforming the chaos of appearance into significant form. It will tend either to "annex" or overrun the world with a multitude of intellectually invented systems of formal and color relationships, or with the equally impersonal and autonomous world of oniric symbols; or else it will slavishly reproduce its chaos.

Contemporary art cannot be said to have come to any such halt. Yet the dangers of its insistence on the absolute autonomy of pictorial values—an insistence derived as much if not more from its rejection of the world as from a positive faith in art—are apparent enough for the artist Malraux to be deeply concerned and to fight them with all his power. Parallel to his "conqueror" metaphysics of art, we find in "Aftermath of the Absolute" a passionate exposition in which he elucidates and helps his fellow artists to unlock his and their very specific prison: the most pervading sense of dread that men may ever have had to face.

> Our consciousness of fate which is as pervading as the Orient's but markedly more animated compares to the fatality of former times as our museum compares to antique collections. Specter of the twentieth century, it has a different size than ghosts of marble. It is against this Specter that the first universal humanism seeks to establish itself.[83]

Universal humanism: by this Malraux, always antihumanist in the specific sense that he rejects the Enlightenment's faith in pure reason and all manifestations of this faith in art and in history, means that our culture is the first to have inherited art in its totality and hence the first to have inherited, in default of a faith, a universal testimony of the "quality of the world."

The rejection of the world of time and place is modern art's major aspect and, as Malraux sets out to show, its major problem. The styles that the artists themselves—rather than the

---

[83] "La Monnaie de l'absolu," *Les Voix du Silence,* p. 629.

art historians—have resurrected and to which they have most avidly turned for guidance, all share a common underlying assumption: that reality lies outside the world of appearances. Sacred and primitive art, children's paintings, and those of schizophrenics, all have this in common, that they testify to something that is irreconcilable with the world and in the light of which the world has been rejected. Yet rejection itself has validity exactly to the extent that it frees an authentic dialogue and makes possible a new relation between the artist and the absolute. This is why the Byzantine mosaics are works of genius and schizophrenic paintings are no art at all, for the latter are based on an involuntary dissociation from the world and reveal nothing but an individual's servitude to the workings of his disrupted psyche. To the mystery of a true conquest they oppose in extreme form an "illusion of miracle," a false epiphany of liberation.

Modern art rejects the world because of the latter's false claim to be the ultimate reality, but it does not reject it in the light of any creative vision of its own. Malraux sees in this rejection a profound sense of distrust and alienation from the world and a need, in the name of a hypothetical value and defense called "pure art," to negate all that exists and to which access has become increasingly difficult.

The existence of "pure painting" can be traced back to Vermeer and it is on the evidence of Vermeer's genius above all that Malraux bases his own theory of art's total freedom and autonomy from any reality outside itself, either supernatural or natural. These paintings do indeed embody a pure quality of transcendence. Yet two things come immediately to mind. The first—and Malraux bears this out—is the extraordinary rarity of such a pure pictorial absolute in the

art of the last centuries; it is a rare miracle of pure poetic
response in which a genius metamorphoses an indifferent
little Dutch world into a timeless, divine realm simply by
imposing on it a quality of infinite harmony and transcendence. And this raises the second point: if Vermeer's art did
"secretly destroy" the world in the sense of destroying its
material autonomy, it thereby transformed it into an image
of eternity. His is a supreme art of transformation. The rela-
tive and specific have indeed been annexed but in a positive
sense. First they have been accepted by the artist as a medium,
a possible realm through which, by his power of metamorphosis, he could elaborate his vision; and secondly, while this
annexation reduced the autonomy of Dutch interiors to nothing, it imposed on them a face of divine nobility. So it would
seem to follow that even a genius who neither affirmed nor
accused fate or the world, but was supremely indifferent to
both, did not create his paintings at the expense of the world.
On the contrary, his paintings related the world itself to a
transcendent reality and delivered it from insignificance.

This becomes exceedingly relevant to Malraux's analysis
of the contemporary situation of art. For here the element
of rejection and destruction which has received such support
in his philosophical synthesis and which we have seen him
emphasize in "The Creative Process" reveals itself as an undisguised danger and temptation. The world has ceased to
be a realm of mediation. It is conceived as a prison and hence
must be destroyed.

Malraux points warningly to the extent to which paint-
ers and sculptors today have rejected the world of man, nature, and objects, and have concentrated on elaborating
"another universe" which is to yield a new fundamental

system of relations. There is on the one hand the cerebral domain of pure research in which all possibilities of construction and stridency, for example, are being investigated; and there is on the other hand the elemental realm of dream and fantasy. Both are highly dangerous, for they not only reveal art's basic loss of reference and its subsequent loss of freedom and vital presence; they also tend to disrupt still further the artist's relation to the world—more essential, even though more difficult, in this sceptical era than ever before—and thereby to endanger his "quality of man" and the "quality of the world."

In the first place, Malraux reminds us, the Manichean split between a sacred or divine absolute on one side and an evil world of reality on the other is Oriental and profoundly contrary to the great art of the West which has striven throughout to humanize the world and draw it into man's dominion.

> To be sure, no style has even served the reality of appearances alone and we have seen why. Even the Mediterranean form of beauty repudiated it in its own way. No less deeply than Hellenism challenged mystery in the name of man, other civilizations have challenged man in the name of eternity or simply of all that was outside man; yet neither death, nor the fascinating descent into the underworld, nor man's attuning himself to all the stars of the night have ever prevailed against the dizzy hope which placed against the palpitating nebula the indomitable little forms of Galilean fishermen or Arcadian shepherds. On the one side are the forms of everything that belongs essentially to man, from feminine beauty to fraternity, from Titian's Venuses to his Pietà; on the other are all those which crush man or elude him, from sphinx to fetish.[84]

[84] *Ibid.*, p. 591.

The unconditional disdain for the world as evidenced by the growing concentration on the totally heterogeneous may become a devouring tide, as he anxiously warns:

> The spread of modern art is accompanied by its growing indifference to the domain which oriented art from the time of the Sumerians until the breaking up of Christendom: the expression of living and dead gods, of the Gospels and of the Fable, the sculptors of the Old Empire, of the Acropolis, the Chinese mountains and the Cathedrals . . . , the painter of the Pietà of Villeneuve and those of the Nara frescoes; Michelangelo, Titian, Rubens, Rembrandt, they all related men to the universe; and even Goya flinging them his dark gifts. Will our art bring them nothing more than the sense of disruption out of which it was born?[85]

Once again, as in the novels, we see Malraux vindicate the human quality revealed by the art of the West above all, against what he recognizes as the true evil. This evil is not the world as such at all. The realm of existence has formed a closely integrated part of at least one of the world's great transcendental cultures; hence it cannot be an intrinsic bar preventing art's access to the absolute. On the contrary, the human face and figure have provided a virtually unlimited range for artistic transfiguration and expressiveness. Their intrinsic mystery allows and calls forth an endless metamorphosis and at the same time their elusiveness and power oppose a hard core of resistance to servile copying on the one hand and to "annexation" or artistic rape—the dissolving of their distinct nature into a purely formal element—on the other.

[85] *Ibid.*, p. 600.

The evil that Malraux sees besieging modern art is precisely the absence or suppression of a specific partner in art's dialogue with fate and the growing number of works that represent an impersonal and unbounded monologue.

On the one side, Malraux unmasks the demon of superrationality which tends to turn abstract art into an art of "annexation" in which a purely formally derived autonomy asserts itself over a universe with which it has not even begun a dialogue. Nothing is really annexed because nothing substantial was challenged in the first place. Such paintings are exactly conquests over nothing and hence represent a fatality instead of a deliverance. This is the danger that abstract art is liable to succumb to if the artist refuses to establish an authentic dialogue with fate on the level of poetic intuition and "invents" his system of pictorial values gratuitously, as it were, on the level of intellectual experimentation.

Malraux's marvelous insight points out the patch as the symbol and principal means of expression of these systems:

> . . . a patch which serves neither the structure of the painting nor its composition in the traditional sense of the term, neither belongs to its treatment nor, as it does in Japan, to its representation; but which seems on the contrary to be its whole *raison d'être,* as if the painting existed only through it. In the works of the painters who first hit upon it one discovers in almost every case that it is related to something: to a fierce constructivism (with Picasso), to an effect of harmony (with Bonnard and later Braque), to an architecture (with Léger). . . . With Miro . . . and also with Klee, the patch is almost autonomous and one is tempted to speak of a one-dimensional art. But it seems to lead the painter toward destroying the very basis of a painting, for

an "absolutely free" art tends to produce not pictures or sculptures, but objects.[86]

And he draws a sad conclusion:

A great artist who, besides knowing the works of our time, knew only the specific plastic qualities of the works of the past would be the supreme incarnation of the modern barbarian; one whose barbarism consists no longer merely of his rejection of the city but of his rejection of the quality of man. If our culture were to consist of nothing but our sensibility to colors and forms and of its valid expression in the contemporary arts, it would be unimaginable.[87]

But there is another temptation to be faced which complements, as it were, that of the intellectual's will-to-autonomy. It is held out by the contemporary demon of irrationality who promises the artist that he will discover the fundamental meaning that he so desperately searches for, in a dark communion with the "night, stars and blood" of the unconscious. Here Malraux's critique becomes scourging. He is utterly hostile to any theory of art which even slightly suggests surrender to impulses, dreams, psychic forces, inspiration of any kind. For this poet of will, art is conquest and achievement, involving the constantly raging battle of "Paul Cézanne against Monsieur Cézanne"[88]; and this, because "men do not find in their cradles nobility of the heart or sanctity or genius, which means that they have to acquire them."[89]

He anxiously and contemptuously questions the illuminations the deeps may yield. "What our anxiety-ridden age is trying to discern in the arts of savages is not only the ex-

[86] *Ibid.*, p. 603.
[87] *Ibid.*, p. 605.
[88] "La Création Artistique," *Les Voix du Silence*, p. 341.
[89] *Ibid.*

pression of another world but also that of those monsters of the abyss which the psychoanalyst fishes for with nets, and politics or war, with dynamite."[90] He warns his fellow artists who are fascinated by African Negro sculpture to the point of having completely pushed aside their own heritage that even those masks—the masks of New Ireland, notably, which suggest man's dispossession of the world by sacred terror— reveal a high artistic self-possession and freedom of response. "We are told that the negro sculptor considers the most effi-cacious mask as the best. What else can account for its efficacy but the density of its style?"[91] The various styles of primitive ancestral masks all belong to an art of iconography which enabled the tribes for whom they were sculpted either to recognize the ancestral figures and transform them into sym-bols or to evoke them magically.

> All of them reveal an imperious presence. Clearly, this presence is the artist's own as always and in even the noblest creations of art, for even the deepest cosmic aware-ness does not suffice to create the style of New Ireland, nor the deepest faith to invent the *Elders* of Moissac. But what this presence implies is the artist's consciousness of the uni-verse . . . a relation which he has established with the cos-mos, not his surrender to it, a conquest and not a sub-servience.[92]

The difference between such a style and the paintings, or at least the theory, of the surrealists becomes apparent. Whereas the first annexes the terrifying god or ancestor to man's domain, the second annexes the human condition to the domain of the unconscious and seeks to establish the

90 "Aftermath of the Absolute," *The Voices of Silence,* p. 575.
91 "La Monnaie de l'absolu," *Les Voix du Silence,* p. 563.
92 *Ibid.,* pp. 568–70.

primacy of dream. Such an endeavor produces one-dimensional monologues of pure psychic "fatality" from which the artist would seem to have disappeared and been replaced by a passive recording machine. The specific "no" inherent in all art has given way here, under the stress of despair, to a total negation both of the human condition and of art's freedom to transform this condition from blind fate to creative self-possession.

Against this total "no" implied by both a purely cerebral and a purely psychological quest, Malraux affirms now once more and with glowing words the continuous reconquest of man and the world which has been and remains the great glory of Western art. Contrary to the great traditions of the Orient and to the primitive arts, all of which have either denied or suppressed the world and conceived man in an absolute confrontation with his gods—expressed by the immobility or rigid movement of sacred or magic ritual—the art of the West has released man's freedom of movement and expression, signs of his infinite mystery, in images that encompass the total range of human response to the absolute, from saturnine despair and Apolline serenity to Christian joy. And it has achieved this by redeeming man's world, that is by acknowledging it as the realm of man's fate and hence as the realm of mediation in which alone the mystery of human freedom can become fully incarnate.

In answer to modern art's struggle to defend itself against dread, Malraux formulates in *The Voices of Silence* what he has elaborated poetically in the novels: namely, the need of accepting the heritage of the past and of recapturing, with its help, a sense of that human quality which in the past has built cathedrals and founded empires. In the present, this

struggle must confine itself to rejecting all that tends to destroy man, above all from within, and to affirm all that may
serve to restore him to self-possession and to a repossession
of the world from which despair has disinherited him. Near
the end of "Aftermath of the Absolute" we read:

> Whether we like it or not the West will elucidate its des-
> tiny only by the light of the torch it is carrying, even if it
> burns its hand: and what this torch seeks to light up is
> everything which can heighten man's power. How can an
> agnostic civilization refuse to have recourse to what has
> transcended it and so often accounted for its greatness?
> If the substance of all culture is the quality of the world,
> its aim is the quality of man. And this it is which makes a
> culture not a *summa* of knowledge but an heir of great-
> ness. Our own artistic culture, knowing that it cannot
> limit itself to the subtle refining of its sensibilities, is grop-
> ing its way in the presence of the figures, songs, and poems
> which constitute the legacy of the world's oldest nobility,
> because it has discovered itself to be today sole heir to that
> bequest.[93]

Formal experimentation and the probing of the deeps may
both well be the means toward achieving this reconquest; on
the condition, however, that the artist does not let himself
be devoured by them but uses them with the single and clear
purpose of regaining and securing more firmly his power of
response.

[93] *Ibid.,* p. 638.

Conclusion

T he new and "as yet indefinable humanism" toward which Malraux seeks to guide his disinherited age in *The Voices of Silence* after having, in the novels, led his heroes out of despair to manhood and to a glimpse of a "mystery" become accessible once again, is not a prophecy. It is less and much more: not a philosopher's exultant assertion claiming for man a divine power and autonomy, but a poet's deeply realized intuition that the artist's power of response which has never failed men in times of anguish will not fail now if he does not surrender to the voices of death.

The nature of this response as he has evolved it in image and exposition lies halfway between total freedom and total servitude, for man is neither fatally delivered to the power of death nor ever free from its menace.

> There is a flaw in us which is sometimes evident and sometimes concealed and against which no god can protect us at all times. The saints call their despair "aridity" and to Christendom the cry "Why hast Thou forsaken me?" is the most human of all cries.[94]

Underlying Malraux's world of distress a profound certainty

[94] "Aftermath of the Absolute," *The Voices of Silence*, p. 628.

153

CONCLUSION 154

is sensed and then becomes evident; namely, that the agony of abandonment can easily mean a condemnation, but that it can also be made to mean a purification and a deepening of man's sense of destiny which will lead him toward a new "mystery" and a more fully realized freedom.

Index

Index